To Doug,

Thank you for buying my book & I hope you enjoy it.

Gid Adkisson

INFANTRY LIEUTENANT

The World War II Memoir of Lieutenant Gid B. Adkisson, Jr.

Able Company, 317th Infantry Regiment,

80th Infantry Division

Gid B. Adkisson, III

Pacifica Military History

INFANTRY LIEUTENANT

The World War II Memoir of Lieutenant Gid B. Adkisson, Jr.

Able Company, 317th Infantry Regiment,

80th Infantry Division

Gid B. Adkisson, III

Gid B. Adkisson, Jr., was one of eight million American men swept into the U.S. Army during the turbulence that was World War II. An earnest West Texas farm boy attending Texas A&M so he could be a better independent farmer, Gid Jr. found himself vying for a lieutenant's commission a full year before he was scheduled to graduate, and fighting in France, Luxembourg, and Germany as an infantry company officer between August 1944 and the end of the war. He was recuperating from his third combat wound when peace finally settled on Europe.

Gid Adkisson, Jr.'s book of war was written by the former lieutenant's oldest child, Gid III, who made it his business to record the war memoir of a man whose preference was to speak and remember little of the war. Thus the book before you is more homage from a proud son than willful memoir from a modest, dutiful man who did his level best to live his life out of the limelight. Along the way, up to and beyond his father's death in 2012, Gid III located and exchanged letters and phone calls with many of the men who served in battle with Gid Jr. in the 80th Infantry Division's Able Company, 317th Infantry Regiment. It was heartwarming to both father and son to learn that Gid Jr. remained in so many *good* memories of an absolutely awful time of life now falling beyond the reach of memory.

ISBN-13: 978-1-58218-8869

Cover Design: Tom Heffron, Hudson Wisconsin
Cover Photo: Official Signal Corps Photo

Please visit http://www.PacificaMilitary.com

Contents

Glossary & Guide to Abbreviations

.45-Caliber pistol Semiautomatic, magazine-fed pistol. Standard issue for army officers. Magazine held seven rounds.

40&8 Train cars common in Europe, capable of carrying 40 people or 8 cows.

Arty Artillery.

BAR Browning Automatic Rifle; 19-pound hand-held machine gun fed by a twenty-round magazine of .30-06 bullets. Each army infantry squad included one BAR man.

Bazooka U.S. shoulder-fired 2.36-inch (60mm) rocket launcher.

Billet Could apply to either a job assignment or housing.

Bivouac Camping area. In military vernacular, can be used as a noun or verb.

Bridgehead Area secured after crossing a river.

Carbine Lighter, smaller variant of the Garand M1 infantry rifle. Used primarily by combat officers, NCOs, and crews of mortars and machine guns during World War II.

CO Commanding officer.

Comm Communications.

CP Command post.

ETO European Theater of Operations.

Exec Executive officer; second in command at the company, battalion, and regimental levels.

FFI French Forces of the Interior, popularly known as the Resistance.

FO Artillery or mortar forward observer.

GI Government Issue; a nickname for all U.S. Army troops

HQ Headquarters.

KP Kitchen police; menial kitchen chores.

M1 Rifle U.S. Garand M1 standard-issue infantry rifle. Semiautomatic, it used a top-fed clip of eight .30-06 rounds. It weighed 9.5 pounds and had a bayonet attachment.

NCO or **Noncom** Noncommissioned officer; corporals and the various grades of sergeant.

OCS Officers Candidate School.

OP Outpost or observation post. Usually two men in a foxhole outside a company perimeter, alert for enemy presence, especially at night.

Pfc Private First Class

POW Prisoner of war.

Replacement Refers to troops who replaced wounded and ill soldiers.

ROTC Reserve Officers Training Corps

S-1, S-3 Staff positions at battalion levels and higher. S-1 was administration; S-3 was operations.

Stage An area designated to set up troops and material prior to an attack or major troop movement.

Table of Organization (TO) "TO strength" refers to the book designation of men and material for a military unit to be at full combat readiness; seldom maintained after theater operations commence.

TD Tank destroyer.

Tech 5 Technician 5th Grade

Preface

Dad told war stories as far back as I can remember. When I was a boy, several of his friends had been in World War II, and our families occasionally shared meals. After everyone had eaten and the table was cleared, the swapping of tales would commence. We children were excused to go play, but I often found a reason to linger around the grown-ups and catch bits of fascinating stories. Movie reels rolled in my mind's eye, as I visualized German soldiers cresting a hill in a head-to-head gun battle, tanks blazing away at each other, and artillery shells blasting enemy strongholds.

The passage of time didn't moderate Dad's telling of stories. When he entered the teaching profession later in life, he found that the promise of a war story at the end of algebra class all but guaranteed an attentive, responsive group of students. Though I never tired of hearing his stories, for many years I more or less took them for granted.

After I retired in 2009, at the suggestion of friends I enrolled in a weekly writing class. While waiting for class to begin one day, I had an epiphany—I needed to compile all of Dad's stories into a book. Within a couple of weeks, I was back on the family farm, sitting next to him, filling cassette after cassette with his stories. By this time, he was 87 and his strength was waning. At this late stage in his life, his war-time experiences seemed to take on renewed significance. He very much wanted this part of his life to be preserved. The forthcoming book would be not just a series of stories, but a part of his legacy.

My intention when I began this project was simple: write and publish a book centered around Dad's ten months as an infantry officer in Europe. As the names of fellow soldiers surfaced during our discussions, I began to locate and contact other survivors; first one, then another, until I had interviewed over the phone or acquired memoirs from ten men who had served with Dad in Able Company, 317th Infantry Regiment. My initial questions to them had to do with recollections of serving with Dad. Some remembered him well, some vaguely, but I quickly learned that each of them had his own war stories. With a little coaxing, I was able to mine some extraordinary accounts from these ordinary men. More than once, pain telegraphed through as they recalled watching helplessly, sixty-five years ago, as a buddy next to them breathed his last.

With each interview, the bank of stories grew. Memories tended to come as individual packages, while the names of towns, dates, and context were often vague or not recalled. Since Dad spent several months in the hospital recuperating from wounds, it seemed fitting to expand the scope of the book to include the accounts of these men, if I could figure out how to piece together their somewhat disconnected recollections.

Thanks to the dedicated efforts of Andy Adkins— whose dad served with my dad—in archiving detailed records of the 80th Infantry Division and posting them on the Internet, I was able to connect almost every story with a date, location, and at least some degree of context. I had access to the morning reports of every company in the 80th Infantry Division as well as interviews with key personnel, citations, and other valuable information. Both Andy's website and Robert Murrell's Operational History of the 80th Infantry Division were invaluable in providing the framework for the stories I recorded.

So I would like to thank Andy and Robert for dedicating a chunk of their lives to the chronicling and publishing of 80th Infantry Division history. Additionally, Andy helped in other ways, including a referral to my publisher, Eric Hammel of Pacifica Military History, without whose guidance and admonitions this would be nothing more than a pamphlet-sized collection of war stories.

I would like also to extend a heart-felt thanks to fellow members of my weekly writing class, who encouraged me along the way and made many helpful suggestions. Without the consistent encouragement of Janice Stevens, our instructor and coach, this work would have never been completed.

** **

Dad passed away on April 24, 2012. My dream was to sit next to him at city hall in the farm town where we both grew up and sign books together, but it was not to be. It was small consolation that he was able to read and approve the manuscript a few months before he left us.

Researching Dad's travels, battles, and the history of the 80th Infantry Division, as well as the first-person accounts of some of his men, took me and this book to places I didn't anticipate. Although I met none of his fellow soldiers face-to-face, I feel a sense of connection to them as well as an obligation to tell their stories as accurately as possible. I hope I have validated their trust.

So, it is to my dad and the men of Able Company, 317th Infantry Regiment, 80th Infantry Division, that I dedicate this book. The importance of keeping the contributions and stories of our veterans has been cited many times in many venues. My hope is that this book will be seen as one of the bricks in the memorial wall that helps preserve the legacy of those who sacrificed so much in the service of their country in World War II.

Thank you, Able Company.
Thank you, Dad.

Above and Beyond the Call of Duty

by
Justin Baca and Cynthia Brooks

The veterans of World War II remain with time tenaciously, although with time the edges of their reminiscences are less sharp and more painful. Now I often talk of these experiences because I believe that this was a time in my life when much of what I have become and who I am was learned. The people and the experiences taught me a great deal about humanity. This story is one of those lessons. I especially want to share it, in order to explain the greatness of one quiet man.

Late September, 1944, in France, was typical of what fall should be. The days were cooler and some of the nights were crisp. I imagine a group of men could have enjoyed a late fall afternoon by the Moselle River. This group was a company of combat infantrymen. I also imagine that these young men were aware of the superb cuisine for which France was so famous. Not so for this unit. We had been subsisting on one K-ration per day for some time.

We were facing the enemy on high ground and had been there for a number of days. Word had just come down that we were about to receive our first hot meal in weeks. Images of turkey legs, thick slices of roast beef with mashed potatoes, and steaming gravy were on every man's mind. Stomachs growled hungrily as we anxiously awaited our feast. When the kitchen crew approached with insulated containers, we cheered them heartily.

At the height of our exuberance, enemy sniper fire sliced the air around us. The bullets sent GIs scurrying for cover, instead of for food. The sniper fire became exceedingly close. The company commander, a salty but caring leader, remarked to his men, "This is the first hot meal we've had in weeks, but, before we eat, let's clean out that sniper's nest, and come back to enjoy our meal in peace!" (At this point, we were on a ridge, with the snipers positioned on a knoll within a clump of trees, just to our right.)

In organizing the attack, the captain had the 2nd and 3rd platoons in frontal attack position, with the 1st--my platoon—in reserve. As the company approached the sniper's nest, the realization came to us that we had surmised the situation all wrong. The closer our troops advanced toward the enemy, the hotter the battle raged. What had been assessed as a small outpost of Germans was actually a full complement of combat soldiers.

The 1st Platoon, led by Lieutenant Gid B. Adkisson, was directed to attack the enemy from the rear flank. The pressure from the frontal assault, plus the added force from the flank, was so intense that the enemy decided to reposition to their rear. In very short order, our adversaries were attempting to break through us, the 1st Platoon, by firing with precision and effectiveness in a running continuous attack. The scene was one of flurried activity and fear. There was firing rapidly and maintaining constant pressure. There were heavy casualties on both sides.

Platoon Leader Adkisson quickly assessed the futility of the situation and the danger to his troops. He elected to cease the offensive and pull back. Word was passed from soldier to soldier and most of what remained of the 1st Platoon reassembled away from the attack position.

Lieutenant Gid became aware that an M1 rifle was still firing continuously and rapidly from the most anterior position that the platoon had reached. He voiced a query, "Who is that firing up there?" Sergeant Joe answered, "I'm not sure, but I think it's Baca."

Now most commanders and most leaders would react to the situation as they had learned at officers' training school: have a noncom carry out the assignment. In this case, to alert the infantry soldier to the change in orders.

Baca had not received the order to pull back because the chain of communication was broken. Two of his buddies on his left, and several to the right, had been fatally wounded. Upon realizing that one of *his* men was in mortal danger, Lieutenant Adkisson spun around and went back to where his rifleman was. Upon reaching a position abreast of Baca, a sudden surge by German soldiers topped the rise, firing perilously. Adkisson and Baca returned the fire, round for round. In the very thick of this battle, the lieutenant's M1 rifle jammed. During a brief lull, Baca glanced up to see who was next to him, and saw that it was his lieutenant.

Adkisson glanced down at his useless weapon in disbelief, then up at the oncoming horde. He threw his rifle to the ground and picked up an enemy submachine gun which lay in front of him. Standing, he and Baca threw out a fusillade of fire that temporarily caused the enemy to fall back. In the brief interlude, the platoon leader bellowed, "We're pulling back! Let's get the hell outa here!"

This brave action saved my life. Lieutenant Gid Adkisson moved far above and beyond the call of duty.

This is only one episode of many in which this man risked his life to save and keep safe *his* men.

Fifty years later, at an 80th Division reunion in Cincinnati, Ohio, we met for the first time in the half century that had elapsed since the end of the war. Together, at a lunch counter we reminisced. He remembered looking down at the rifled that had jammed. But that was all he remembered. Not a thought had been given to the extreme danger he had placed himself in. There had been no regard to the great self risk and jeopardy to himself. The awesomeness of this action is indescribable. Words fail. That late afternoon in France, an everlasting bond was established between two men.

Chapter 1
From the Farm to Aggieland
July 30, 1922–July 12, 1943

I was enjoying a pick-up game of basketball in the college gym on December 7, 1941, when our maid burst through the door. "The Japs have bombed Pearl Harbor and the President has declared war."

I was in my sophomore year at Texas A&M (Agricultural & Mechanical) College in College Station, Texas. The outbreak of war with the Japanese, followed by a declaration of war from Hitler a few days later, meant that I and all of my fellow students who were physically qualified were going to dedicate a chunk of our lives to Uncle Sam, regardless of our original intent when we enrolled in college.

My initial reason for attending the school had little to do with the potential of a military career, let alone going overseas to fight in a war. My goal in life was to be a farmer, and I was at A&M as a result of a deal I had worked out with my father.

**

My paternal grandfather, Gideon Joseph Adkisson, was from Tennessee, and served as a captain for the South in the Tennessee cavalry in the Civil War. According to family lore, not long after the war, a dispute, the nature of which remains a mystery, arose between my grandfather and another man. It was serious enough that Grandpa Gideon ultimately shot and killed the man in self-defense. As the story goes, the local sheriff, aware of the circumstances, got wind of planned retaliation by the dead man's family and paid a late-night visit to my grandfather. The sheriff apprised him of the scheme, and told him that he did not have adequate manpower to provide protection. The only way to assure his safety was for him to leave town without delay. My grandfather, who was single, had relatives in Texas, so he hastily

1

packed his belongings and began the long westward trek to start life anew.

He traveled to La Grange, in southeast Texas, where he met and eventually married Tabitha Moore, niece of Colonel John Henry Moore, a Texas pioneer who had achieved considerable fame by leading a contingent of troops to victory at the Battle of Gonzales in October 1835. It was actually more of a skirmish but was significant in that it signaled the beginning of Texas' fight for independence from Mexico.

Gideon and Tabitha had two girls and three boys, and after relocating for a short time to nearby Pflugerville, left the area and moved north into the Panhandle, where they put down roots on a farm near Memphis, east of Amarillo.

My father, Gideon Bowen Adkisson, was born in 1878. He spent his early years following in his father's footsteps, plowing behind a team in flat, dry West Texas. In his late twenties, his relationship with a childhood friend, Nellie Eichelberger, who was several years his junior, blossomed into romance. Although her father could make himself quite a public nuisance when he was in his cups, she had a calm demeanor and sweet spirit, which won my father's heart. They became husband and wife in 1906.

Nellie and Gideon moved to Lakeview, a few miles west of Memphis, and started a family. Their first child was Jo Dolph, followed by Douglas, then Roy, and then two girls, Ella B. and Alice. Roy came down with diphtheria the day after he started grade school and died within a few days. My mother never completely recovered from losing her young son.

In 1918, lured by cheap land prices and unbroken prairie, my father bought a section of land near Abernathy. He built a house and barn, dug a well, and erected a windmill to pump the water. He broke the land and planted cotton, milo, and wheat, and he was successful enough that he was able to become a partner in the ownership of a couple of buildings in the young community, including the local bank building.

I came along six and a half years after Alice, in July, 1922, the only child born after the move to Abernathy. I don't know if I was planned or not, but it is a moot point, because I had a great life. I was treated as an only son; I had two sisters who doted on me, and I loved every aspect of farm life.

2

As a boy, I made the three-mile trip to school either on horseback or in the family buggy, toting my schoolbooks and a lunch consisting of two my of mother's sausage and biscuit sandwiches, wrapped in newspaper. The kids who lived in town loved those sandwiches, so bartering for lunches was a daily occurrence. When I was in third grade, my dad bought a Model A Ford, which got me to school faster and more comfortably.

Every year I was given more chores to perform, mostly related to working with the livestock. At age eleven, I had a sort of rite of passage. That was the year my father allowed me to start plowing with our two-horse team, Dolly and Dan. In spite of my string-bean physique, I was able to control them and get the job done. Most of all, I was doing a man's work.

By the time I was in seventh grade, I was helping to milk eighteen cows before breakfast. We sold the milk to the local creamery in town, which provided a monthly stipend to supplement our once-a-year crop income.

That same year, my dad gave me a heifer to use as a source of personal income. I took good care of her, and when she was mature enough to produce, began selling her milk along with that of our small herd. I saved the money I earned until I had enough to buy a second heifer, eventually doubling my milk income. It felt good to be earning my own spending money.

The milk money not only gave me some financial independence, it also paid my way to a special event. In 1936, there was a centennial celebration in the Dallas–Ft. Worth area. Several of my classmates and I made the trip to the big event, my first time away from home. We had a great time and I remember being fascinated as we toured the local Ford Motor Company plant and watched cars being assembled.

There were breaks from the work routine of the farm. Quite often on Saturday afternoons, my parents went to town to shop while I met my school friends at the theater to watch the free Saturday matinee. Sunday afternoons during the summer, my mother packed a lunch and we drove the ten miles in our Model A to the Tuco cotton gin lot, where my dad played catcher in a local softball league. The shopping trips and softball games were major social events.

3

One of my fondest childhood memories, ranking just behind Christmas, was hog-killing time. Farmers raised livestock to provide meat for their families, which meant the animals had to be slaughtered and butchered. Processing hogs required a scalding vat, the nearest one of which was several miles away. One year, my father took the initiative to build such a vat and thus established our farm as the hog-killing site for a half-dozen neighboring farmers. The first year was such a success that an annual fall tradition was established. Fathers and sons set up a sort of assembly line, with everyone participating. My job initially was to scrape all the hair off of the carcasses after they were scalded, and I progressed from there.

The wives and daughters prepared their specialty dishes and brought them to the house, providing us with a veritable feast at the end of the day, highlighted by my mother's unsurpassed blackberry cobbler for dessert. It was a festive time, at least for the humans.

**

Times were lean, but since everyone was in the same boat, I never really felt deprived. People were resourceful and learned to get by. On our infrequent trips to Lubbock, Jo Dolph and Douglas brought along the single-shot .22-caliber rifle and watched for rabbits as we drove. When they spotted one, Dad pulled over and stopped the car, and the boys took a shot. They usually bagged a couple in the course of the forty-mile round trip, which meant we were having rabbit stew for supper—not exactly a delicacy, but the price was right.

While our fortunes were slim in the early 1930s, they took a distinct turn for the better in 1937. We had a bountiful milo crop, and prices were good. In 1938, we converted our earnings into some current-day luxuries. We tied into the new electrical grid and my dad bought a refrigerator and electric washing machine, freeing my mother from the drudgery of a using a scrub board, and allowing me to do homework by the light of an electric bulb instead of a coal oil lamp. We also installed an indoor toilet. To top it off, we bought a new four-door Chevrolet, nicer by far than any car I had ever ridden in.

That summer, instead of telling me where to plow, my dad asked me where I thought I should plow. He told me it would be my decision the following spring as to what crops would be planted in different fields, which was an encouraging vote of confidence. By this time we owned a tractor and modern, two-row equipment, and my dream of becoming a farmer was coming into view.

Not only were things shaping up well on the farm scene, my social life was good. I had plenty of friends, and was dating a really nice girl. At six feet, two inches and one hundred sixty pounds, I made the varsity basketball team my junior and senior years. My senior year in high school, I was voted class favorite.

**

At about the time of spring planting in 1940, my dad eased a monkey wrench into my plans when he broached the subject of college. Neither of my brothers had furthered their education beyond high school, but both of my sisters had earned degrees. I felt that I was building momentum towards running the family farm and was planning accordingly, so I initially objected. But after quasi-negotiations (he was the undisputed head of the household, so I didn't push back very hard), I agreed to a year's enrollment and chose Texas A&M because of its agricultural orientation. I matriculated in the fall of 1940, fully expecting to be back in Abernathy at the end of the first year after paying my dues. By the time I came home for Thanksgiving, however, I was a died-in-the-wool Aggie. There was no turning back.

**

I was in the class of 1944. A&M was a military school, established with a state grant in 1876. Although not an official military academy, such as West Point, it essentially functioned as such with an all-male student body and all but a few students enrolled in the cadet corps. Many A&M graduates served in the armed forces after graduation, especially during the World War II years. Texas A&M supplied twenty thousand combat troops for the war effort, more than fourteen thousand of whom became officers. This was more than any other educational institution in the nation, including West Point and Annapolis.

Cadets lived in dormitories, segregated by company and battalion. Uniforms were worn seven days a week and formations were held morning and night, as we marched to the mess hall for chow. Many of our Saturday mornings were devoted to close-order drill. On occasion, a visiting dignitary would be of sufficient status to merit having the entire cadet corps pass in review in dress uniforms. Membership in the cadet corps and the study of military science were mandatory during one's freshman and sophomore years. During our junior and senior years, students had the option of signing a military contract to make them official members of the Reserve Officers Training Corps (ROTC), for which they earned the sum of twenty-five cents per day.

As with other military schools, A&M was steeped in tradition. An elaborate system of privileges evolved based on class standing. Hazing, including calisthenics in a hallway or the privacy of an upperclassman's room; impromptu inspections; and constant "chewing out" were all a part of a freshman's daily life. Seniors had wooden paddles large enough to be grasped with two hands that were used for the purpose of dispensing discipline as was deemed appropriate. Freshmen and an occasional sophomore who committed an infraction were routinely called into a senior's room and made to bend over to submit to a few whacks across the bottom with the paddle, or sometimes two paddles when each of two seniors positioned themselves on either side of the offender and "drove stakes."

The "maid" I referred to was not a nice lady with a scarf in her hair. All single students lived on campus in two-man rooms. It was a sophomore privilege to have a freshman come in at an appointed time and clean his room every day, hence the term "maid." Freshmen had few privileges. They were never addressed by first name. They were all known as "Fish," as in Fish Adams, Fish Johnson, Fish Davidson, Fish Adkisson, etc.

Those of us who made it through freshmen year developed thick skin, both literally and figuratively. Indeed, anyone who graduated from Texas A&M had endured a tough grind beyond academics in many ways. The result was, as our careers in the real army unfolded, Aggies were not intimidated by the standard fare of a military environment, such as rank structure, passing inspections, military discipline, or fear of offending a superior.

6

I had never spent time away from home or been exposed to anything other than farm life. Thus my time at A&M was an eye-opening experience. A&M was more than just a college. It was a brotherhood, a huge fraternity, and I thrived on the camaraderie and esprit de corps. Not everyone was suited for such an environment, but for those who were, there was a strong sense of pride and loyalty to school, cadet corps, and fellow students. Each year brought a new level of privileges and responsibilities as upperclassmen oversaw the conduct and development of those who followed them. When the chips were down, Aggies stuck together, regardless of class or rank. I readily acknowledge that this was one of the most positive and formative experiences of my life. I had learned responsibility at home, but it was taken to a new level while I was a member of the cadet corps. I learned to endure hardship and, most importantly, how to lead men, especially as commanding officer of my cadet company during my senior year. I loved my school and my fellow cadets.

The entire country was deeply enmeshed in World War II throughout most of my college years. The officials at A&M knew that all contract cadets enrolled during a time of war would ultimately end up in military service, so they instituted a "speed-up" program to enable as many young men as possible to receive a degree before reporting for duty. The school was on the semester system. At the end of my sophomore year, June 1942, my class immediately began our junior year instead of having the summer off. This meant that our junior year ended in January 1943, again followed by commencement of our senior year with no break. In February 1943, the army called to active duty all contracted members of the junior and senior classes. We were to be sent to reception centers for initial processing into the army, followed by Officers Candidate School (OCS), and field assignments. A&M administrators negotiated a deal with the army to allow us to interrupt our studies for a week, go through this induction process, then return to the campus to finish the semester (now crammed into an eight-week course) before becoming official government property.

Induction: March 1943

About six hundred A&M juniors and seniors reported to various induction centers for the agreed-on processing. Along with four hundred others, I reported to Fort Sam Houston in San Antonio, Texas. The noncommissioned officers at "Fort Sam" didn't know it, but they were about to be introduced to a different breed of recruit than they had seen before.

We were responsible for our own transportation to and from the induction center. We all reported by 0900 on a Monday during the first week of March. Though we were well on our way to earning college degrees at this point, as far as the army was concerned, we were buck privates. On arrival, we were shown to our barracks, each housing about sixty men, and then directed to a supply warehouse at which we were issued uniforms. Next was a trip to the barber shop. After getting haircuts, we returned to our barracks to drop off our gear and await further instructions.

Before long, a veteran NCO strode into the barracks. He was five feet, ten inches tall and in his early thirties. His khaki uniform was crisp; he had good military bearing; and he was a bit smug, but not arrogant. A "lifer" for sure. His normal routine was to take eighteen-year-old raw civilian recruits and give them their very first taste of life as a soldier in the United States Army. He had done this so many times that he could have sleepwalked through his routine. He approached us in the same manner as he had approached countless others before: he called us outside and positioned himself in front of us, then issued the standard order, "Fall In." He naturally expected the usual stumbling and confusion, which would give him the satisfaction of emphatically pointing out deficiencies and hopeless incompetence while lamenting the future of the armed forces and the American war effort.

To his astonishment, we all fell into three straight—neat ranks, dressed right—and came to perfect attention in a platoon formation, thumbs along trouser seams, all eyes straight ahead. The sergeant was taken aback, but he regained his composure and prepared to march us to chow. The sergeant had us do a "left face" and "forward march." The mess hall was in plain sight of all hands,

8

and it was obvious that we would march to the end of the street, execute a "column right," go a short distance, and be given the command to "halt" in front of the building. As we reached the end of the street, the sergeant gave the command, "column left." True to our training, we followed orders. The sergeant, not yet adjusted to this group of not-so-raw recruits, became flustered and barked, "No, damn it, I meant 'column right.'" We started a column right, placing the first few men in the middle of the flower beds within a few paces. In exasperation he yelled, "STOP!" Dropping all military protocol, he finally said, "You all know where the mess hall is. Go get something to eat." He walked over to examine the damage to the flowers as we sauntered into the chow hall. After lunch, we returned to the barracks.

We hadn't been in the barracks long before the sergeant reappeared to issue further orders. "Okay, gentlemen, we are going to have what is known in the army as a 'field day,'" which was nothing new to Aggies. "That means I want these barracks to be scrubbed from top to bottom. There are some GI brushes in the latrine. I will be back in a few hours to inspect." Following his departure, a discussion ensued in our ranks as to whether we should comply with this order or not, and what other options we might have. My roommate, Ike McCarroll, had been issued a fatigue jacket with corporal's stripes painted on the sleeve. Another classmate, Cullen Rogers, who had been a starting halfback on the A&M football team, said, "I've got an idea. Ike. Give me that jacket. I think I can take care of this situation." He put on the jacket and went for a walk down the company street. He soon chanced upon a couple of recruits fresh off the farm and stopped them. Pointing to the sleeve, he said, "Do you men know what these stripes mean?"

Wide-eyed, they responded, "Yes, sir."

"Come with me, I have a job for you." They obediently followed him to our barracks. He informed them that their assignment for the afternoon was to thoroughly clean the barracks. "By the way," he added, "these men have been on an all-night training exercise and are very tired. Work quietly so they can get some rest." Thereupon, most of us settled into our racks for afternoon naps.

After the two boobs had finished, Rogers inspected their work and had them clean the latrine a second time before dismissing them. They left just before the sergeant returned to conduct his inspection. After a thorough tour, he assembled us and issued his verdict, "You men have done a good job. Go ahead and take the rest of the afternoon off."

We completed our induction process by week's end, returned to the A&M campus, and finished our semester of study. The educational endeavors for our two classes were now put on indefinite hold as we transitioned to full-time military service. I, along with my fellow seniors, was one semester away from receiving my degree. Under normal conditions, my A&M classmates and I would not attend OCS. We would have attended army boot camp during the summer between our junior and senior years, and, upon graduation from college the next year, would have pinned on our second lieutenant bars. The war and speed-up program changed all of that.

Following a brief break, we returned to Fort Sam Houston as buck privates to await openings for our first official training as GIs. As a future infantry officer, I would be reporting to OCS at Ft. Benning, Georgia, when enough men had been accumulated in the queue to form a class. As it turned out, our time at Ft. Sam became a classic military holding pattern that lasted eight weeks, which I am sure was as trying for the noncoms, who were essentially babysitting, as it was for us.

Hurry Up and Wait

This time around, we were under the command of a first sergeant whose education, by our estimation, maxed out at the eighth-grade level, and who made it clear from the outset that he did not like "college boys." He was a short man with the persona of a bantam rooster. He seemed to operate under the incorrect assumption that the louder he shouted, the more intimidated we would be. He was more of an irritant than anything else and got little more than dutiful obedience out of us.

Our introduction to the first sergeant began with a lecture on maintaining our living area. Probably due to his stature, he usually spoke from a platform when addressing his troops. In our first orientation meeting, he stepped onto his platform and reviewed the standards for each man's area. The barracks consisted of a fairly long corridor with bunk beds lined up facing each wall and an aisle in between. Every bunk had two shelves mounted on the wall at the head. His instruction concerning the use of the shelves was simple: "I don't want nothing on them there shelves, and what is there had better be neat." He looked a bit puzzled as a ripple of chuckles went through the ranks.

Also included in our group of overseers was a corporal who had attended A&M for a couple of years with some of the men. He had dropped out to join the army and was familiar with our background, traditions, training, and so forth. The first sergeant and other NCOs were somewhat perplexed when they observed us instantly complying with instructions from the corporal while seeming to grudgingly tolerate their own leadership efforts.

By the last two weeks of our stay, our ranks had dwindled down to only a hundred or so men who had not yet shipped out. Looking for ways to get out of the barracks and away from trivial duties, we conspired with the corporal to institute daily training hikes, made with the blessing of the first sergeant and other noncoms. What the upper echelons didn't know was that we had also conspired with the corporal and a local bakery and a dairy distributor to meet us every afternoon a couple of miles away from the base with vans laden with pastries and dairy treats. After a long, leisurely snack time, we all hiked back to the base. The staff kept waiting to hear complaints about the daily hikes, but none were forthcoming.

Chapter 2
Training to Lead
July 12, 1943–November 20, 1943

Assignments finally arrived for those of us remaining at Ft. Sam Houston. It was time for us to exit our holding pattern and board the train for a three-day trip to Ft. Benning, Georgia, where we would begin our official military careers. It was now mid-July 1943.

The train, pulled by a coal-burning engine, was hot and uncomfortable. We alternated between leaving the windows open for fresh air, which drew in hot cinders from the engine, and leaving them closed, which eliminated the cinders but subjected us to stifling heat. It was a long three days.

To provide some rest and relief, I found that I could take the back off of a seat, lay it in the aisle, and use it for a mattress during the night. The second night of the trip, someone traversing the aisle accidentally stepped on my face, leaving a scratch and a bruise.

My first memory on reporting in to Ft. Benning was a thorough questioning by a lieutenant as to why my face was bruised. I explained what had happened to the lieutenant's satisfaction and was allowed to proceed. Anyone who got into a fight at OCS was automatically terminated from the program.

Army OCS, seventeen weeks in duration, was both a training course and weeding-out process. The objective was to take officer candidates, most of whom were college graduates or only a few units shy of a degree, and turn them into infantry platoon leaders. Upon arrival, we were all assigned the rank and pay grade of corporal. We went through a battery of tests and orientation briefings. One somewhat surprising statistic was that the army had a surplus of thirty thousand infantry officers, which meant that many of the men who began the course would not receive commissions.

OCS was competitive, and, while we naturally made friends and pulled for each other, the system mitigated against becoming too close to other candidates. Much weight was given to peer evaluations. We periodically rated each other in different groups. Not only was the evaluation considered, but also the judgment of the evaluator. If a candidate rated an underperforming platoon member well, it could be an indication of poor judgment by the person doing the evaluation, and thus would be a detriment. It was not an "every man for himself" environment, but we were all aware that we would be called on to scrutinize each other. The army had worked out a somewhat stealthy disqualification procedure. When someone was cut from the program, not much was said about it. We just came in from maneuvers and the disqualified man was gone, along with all of his gear. No good-byes, handshakes, or other formalities. They were there one day and gone the next.

After a few weeks, we began to get Saturday night and Sunday off, and would go into town. Several of us found a good steak house, which became our hangout. It looked like a dump, but they had good food, and especially good steaks. Everyone was focused on making it through the program, so I don't remember us carousing or doing anything that would jeopardize our chances for graduation.

My bunkmate was Andy Adkins, a graduate of The Citadel, a military school located in Charleston, South Carolina. Like me, Andy had been in the cadet corps, so we had a similar background and adapted quickly to the military environment. We occasionally compared notes on school traditions and who had suffered the most during our freshman year of college, and which institution was most hallowed. But mostly we focused on getting through the program. I remember that he was very smart, had a very dry wit, and could see some degree of humor in just about everything.

Courses of instruction included maneuvers from squad to company level. The staple of the infantry at that time was the M1 rifle, so we qualified with this and the .45-caliber pistol. In addition, we either received training or did familiarization firing on every weapon used by the army, up to and including the 105mm howitzer. I remember being impressed by the fact that, standing alongside the 105 and sighting along the barrel, I could actually see the 105 round for the first half second or so of its flight.

We experienced quite a scare during one of our training sessions. We were all settled into bleachers to receive introductory training on the fine art of throwing hand grenades. The instructing officer showed us the two different types of grenades that would be used in training. Exhibit A was a practice grenade that was painted bright red. When the pin was pulled and the spring-loaded handle, made of light-weight molded tin, was released, there was a three-second delay, and then the grenade would pop. It was harmless. He then held up Exhibit B, a live grenade, olive drab in color with small metal squares. It resembled a miniature pineapple with a handle at the top. He held the grenade above his head, making sure all of us could see it, brought it down to chest level, and, with a bit of flair, pulled the pin. "Then you throw the grenade, duck for cover, and three seconds later . . . BOOM! You hope to have fewer Germans to worry about." Then, as he attempted to casually reinsert the pin, we heard, "Oh my God." and a "ping" sound as the spring-loaded handle flew off. As the grenade dropped to the ground, we all instinctively scattered in every direction, leaping over the bleacher railings, scrambling for safety. We waited a few tense seconds for the inevitable, then finally began to look around cautiously, concluding that there was not going to be an explosion. "Okay, everybody back in your seats," the officer called, as he picked up the weapon with a grin on his face. "I just wanted to make sure I have your full attention." It wasn't nearly as funny to us as it was to him, but his little prank had the desired effect.

One other instructor, teaching a leadership course, left an indelible, though somewhat benign, mark on the class. The instructor was giving examples of how a young lieutenant could evaluate his effectiveness as a leader. One such example had to do with subordinates' responses to orders issued under combat conditions. If a lieutenant told a squad leader to get his men together to embark on a risky mission and the men carried out the assignment without question, the lieutenant could be reasonably assured that his men respected him as a leader. On the other hand, if the men under his command did not respect his leadership abilities, given the same situation, the squad leader would listen to the order, walk away saying, "Piss on you, cowboy," and try to figure out a way around it. After that, the standard retort among all of us officer candidates to any advice or requests from our peers was nothing less than, "Piss on you, cowboy."

One of my achievements in OCS was that I managed to singlehandedly shut down a company-sized live-fire exercise, at least temporarily. It was early fall and we were fairly well along in the program. Per the now-familiar routine, we were trucked out to our training area one morning to begin platoon exercises. We were required to shave every day, and for some reason, on this particular morning, I had run out of time early in the morning and had to choose between shaving and being late to formation. I grabbed my razor, dropped it into my pocket, and made it to the noon hour without my unshaven condition being detected. We had K-rations for lunch, but I moved to an inconspicuous position while everyone was chowing down, splashed some water from my canteen on my face, quickly shaved, and put the razor back in my pocket. We assembled at 1300 and received a briefing on the live-fire maneuver we were going to execute. A captain was in charge, and he was emphatic that we stay low and maintain strict safety standards. They wanted us to get a feel for live rounds overhead, but, while sustaining casualties in a training maneuver might have been realistic, that was way beyond the objective and would certainly have marked the end of the captain's career in the army. We got into position and moved out, all under close supervision. Without thinking, I reached into my pocket for something and cut my thumb on the razor. It began to bleed, but I continued to focus on our objective, aiming and firing as we moved. I was unaware that blood was now running down my cheek. Suddenly one of the referees, another captain, shouted, "Cease fire, cease fire," and ran towards me.

My first impulse was to think, "Why is he running towards me? What have I done? I'm doing everything exactly as instructed."

"Are you okay, candidate?" he asked. "Where is that blood coming from? Have you been hit?"

I looked down at my thumb, ran my finger across my cheek, and realized what had happened. "No, sir. I cut my thumb but didn't realize I was bleeding."

15

Assured that I had not been wounded, we resumed the maneuver. I made a mental note to never carry a razor with the blade in it in my pocket again.

**

Job responsibilities—billets—were rotated regularly to give us a variety of leadership opportunities as well as expose us to various military responsibilities. Billets were posted on the company bulletin board every three days. The rumor was that if someone was posted to the same billet twice in a row, he had better ramp up his efforts, because that was an indication of marginal performance and a precursor to dismissal from the program. With two weeks of OCS remaining, I saw that I was assigned as company commander. I had been a company commander at Texas A&M, so the title and weight of the position were not new to me, but I did not want to come this close to graduation and run into a problem. After three days in the billet, I checked the roster to see what my new assignment might be, if I had one at all. To my surprise and concern, my name was on the roster for a second cycle as company commander. Then again, three days later, the same thing. I remained as a somewhat nervous company commander until I was relieved by one of the staff officers just prior to marching to graduation ceremonies. After graduation, I asked the CO why I had been left as company commander. His answer was that I had a voice that everyone could hear and I didn't make mistakes, so they left me in that billet.

As predicted during our early briefings, of the 220 men in our group who began the program, only 104 received commissions.

It was November 1943. I was entitled to two weeks' leave before reporting to my first assignment as a second lieutenant in Yuma, Arizona. Before Yuma, however, I had a very important matter to attend to.

Chapter 3
Tying the Knot
November 20, 1943–December 10 1943

A year earlier, I had met a coed who was attending Texas Tech College in Lubbock, Texas. She was from Quitaque, Texas, a small farm town not far from Lubbock, and her name was Marie Hall. We met on a blind date while I was home from A&M for the Christmas holidays during my junior year. We hit it off immediately and she flirted with me the whole night. Actually, it was a double date that my old high school buddy, Troy Williams, had arranged. He and Marie had been dating casually and she had set me up with one of the girls in the boarding house where she lived. My date was a pretty girl and very nice, but not much of a talker. Marie, on the other hand, was not only attractive; she was lively, outgoing, and had a great sense of humor. There was immediate chemistry between us. The fact that I wore my dress uniform probably didn't hurt my cause. We laughed and teased each other as much as we dared without being downright rude to our respective dates. In the course of the evening, she told me that she worked at Broome Optical part time.

The next afternoon found me standing in front of her work desk asking for her address, which she willingly gave me in exchange for mine. We began writing to each other as soon as I got back to school. The letters quickly progressed from newsy and chatty to a more endearing tone. In the spring, I invited her down for the senior ring dance, a five-hundred mile trip one way by train. We had a wonderful time. By now, there was no question in my mind that this was the woman I wanted to marry. I composed a proposal letter and dropped it in the mail. And then I waited.

After several days, I received a reply of "Yes," and we were officially engaged. Her mind had long since been made up and she said later that she "just about broke my neck getting to the post office to get a return letter in the mail." A wedding date was set for

17

Thanksgiving, assuming the government did not interfere with our plans. There were no guarantees, and I wanted to make sure that I had my bars and knew my assignment before we made a life-long commitment.

So, the time for our wedding had arrived. The plan was for us to meet in New Orleans, where we would exchange vows, then travel back to West Texas for a brief stay before I reported to Yuma. We arrived in New Orleans from opposite directions and went together to the mayor's office to obtain a marriage license, where we discovered that there was a small problem. Marie was only twenty years old, one year shy of the requirement for marriage without parental permission. She had a letter in hand from her mother that granted her permission to wed, but it was not notarized. A lady in the office took up our cause. After hearing our story and reading the letter, she walked out into a hallway, found two uniformed policemen, and brought them into the office. She introduced them to us and asked, "Doesn't this woman look twenty-one years old to you?" They both agreed that there was little doubt that she was at least twenty-one years old. They signed forms attesting to that fact, and the matter was settled. We wanted to be married by a Methodist minister, if possible. The lady again came to our aid by locating a Methodist minister, who volunteered to perform the marriage ceremony in his home. We got directions and took a taxi to the home, where we exchanged wedding vows. There might be grounds for concern regarding the legitimacy of the union, however. The law required two adults to witness the ceremony for the bond to be legal. The minister's adult daughter was a witness, but his wife was upstairs sick in bed. The legal wedding document was taken up to her room for her to sign, after which we went on our way. Sixty-six years, six children, and many grandchildren later, it is probably a moot point.

After a couple of days in New Orleans, we boarded a bus for West Texas. I was entitled to two weeks' leave before reporting for my first assignment as a second lieutenant.

Chapter 4
Preparing for War
December 10, 1943–August 6, 1944

I was assigned to the 80th Infantry Division, which was training in the Arizona desert. The 80th Division was first established August 5, 1917, in the National Army, headquartered at Camp Lee, Virginia, and began preparation for service in World War I. The division logo had three blue mountain peaks as a background, symbolizing the states of Pennsylvania, Virginia, and West Virginia. It was nicknamed the "Blue Ridge Division."

After training at Camp Lee for nine months, the division, 23,000 strong, set sail for France, with the final elements landing during the first week of June 1918. After serving with distinction, the 80th returned to the States in May 1919 and was deactivated at Camp Lee on June 26, 1919.

Twenty-three years later, on July 15, 1942, the 80th Division was resurrected and, again, was populated primarily by men from the eastern part of the country. Major General Joseph Dorch Patch, the division commanding general, issued General Order No. 1 to reactivate the division. Brigadier General Horace McBride, who had served briefly with the unit in the World War I, became the artillery commander. The division formed up and began training in Camp Forrest, Tennessee. The next phase of training was conducted at Camp Phillips, Kansas, followed by the final phase carried out in the California–Arizona Desert Training Center, which was known as Camp Laguna. In March 1943, General McBride became the commanding general of the division, who became one of only two U.S. Army division commanders in World War II who trained and continued on through the entire war with the same outfit.

Arizona, Mid December 1944

Camp Laguna, located about thirty miles northeast of Yuma, was a tent city established strictly for army training purposes. It was very primitive with no permanent structures, no electricity, and no running water, just sand and cactus as far as the eye could see. We were there to be trained to work together as a unit from platoon up to division level.

I was assigned as platoon leader for the 1st Platoon, A (Able) Company, 1st Battalion, 317th Infantry Regiment. With quite a bit of leadership experience under my belt from my days at A&M, I was not lacking in confidence, but I was aware that I would have to earn the trust and confidence of my men, most of whom were from Blue Ridge states. Quite a few were older than me. I found out well into our training that, when I took over, I was referred to among the troops as "that tall, skinny kid from Texas." That could probably be construed to indicate skepticism, but I like to think that, as they looked back on their time in combat, their trust was well placed.

My platoon sergeant was Johnny Fabrizio, a technical sergeant from Akron, Ohio. He had already been in the army for three years. Johnny was married but had no children. He had trained with the regiment in Tennessee, so was a bona fide old timer. Standing five feet, eight inches tall, with dark hair and a somewhat slight build, he was three years my senior, which did not seem to affect him at all. He was personable, the kind of man who liked people, and it showed in the way he handled the troops. We thought a lot alike and quickly became a good team.

The tent city was our home for the entire stay in Arizona. It had none of the comforts of life except for the occasional one-day leave for trips into Yuma.

The desert offered its unique set of challenges. We had to be on the lookout for snakes and scorpions, and even the cactus plants. There were native cactus plants scattered around that had balls hanging from them with fishhook needles. Once they got caught on your clothing, they were difficult to get off without tearing something, including your skin. They even penetrated the tops of our leather boots. We learned to stay clear of these annoying plants.

There were also pack rats, which looked like miniature kangaroos. They came in at night and stole anything they could carry, especially anything shiny. I don't remember losing anything, but I did wake up a few times to find my boots in a different place than I left them.

If the wind blew at all when we were on maneuvers, we found little sand dunes in the middle of our tents when we returned.

It was also very, very hot during daytime. The men had to be careful not to get dehydrated, especially on hikes where they were dependent on canteen water. It was so hot that if they got in early enough from maneuvers to wash their clothes and hang them on their tent ropes, the clothes would be completely dry before dark. When the sun went down, so did the temperature. In the late spring, we were sleeping under two woolen blankets.

We slept on cots, and the officers lived two or three to a tent. My first tent mate was Lieutenant Allen. He was from a wealthy family and knew how to take good care of himself. He had acquired a small gasoline lantern that he lit one night to generate some heat in the tent. This was fine with me, but what wasn't fine was that he had placed the lamp right under my Class A uniform, which was hanging from the ceiling. I smelled something funny and looked up to see the bottom my uniform beginning to smoke. I reacted quickly and saved my uniform and extinguished his lantern in the process. He couldn't understand why I made such a big deal of it, and his lantern never was quite the same. He was transferred to another division not long afterward. My next tent mate was much more compatible.

Desert training was demanding. We were routinely pushed to the limit of our physical endurance. One time, I was so exhausted that I fell asleep on my feet while walking down a road during a battalion movement. I woke up when I bumped into Sergeant Fabrizio, who started to give me a hard time about it. I told him that I was just checking on him. We accumulated so many miles of marching and maneuvering in the gritty sand that I wore out four pairs of size-13 boots in four months. The sand just ate them up.

Each of the lieutenants was responsible for some aspect of our training. I taught bayonet fighting and hand-to-hand combat. I took the training we had received at OCS, improvised a bit, and came up with a course of instruction. By the time our training in Yuma was finished, I felt pretty confident about my odds of winning in just about any hand-to-hand combat situation.

One of our last exercises was a one-day thirty-five-mile hike. By the end of the hike, we were all so exhausted that when we reached our destination, we laid down on the ground and went to sleep. Sergeant Fabrizio and I each carried an extra pack for the last ten miles; we had two men who just couldn't make it without help.

Observations From Pfc Justin Baca

When Lieutenant Adkisson reported, most of the men in our platoon were skeptical. He was a college kid, another 90-day wonder, and we assumed he would be just like many of the other lieutenants we had encountered. They often communicated in various ways that they were superior to us. "Rank hath its privileges." And many exercised their rank by having enlisted men do things that they would not do themselves. As time went on, Lieutenant Adkisson made it clear by his actions that he did not consider himself to be better than us, nor did he expect us to do anything that he would not do.

I remember one evening early on, when we embarked on a hike that took a good part of the night. As the miles wore on, men began to wear out and lag behind. Not only was he in better shape than most of the platoon, instead of barking orders at the men who were struggling, he came alongside of them and encouraged them to keep going. It was not uncommon for him to take the pack of a straggler during marches and carry it himself. He never belittled or talked down to his troops, either one-on-one, or in a group.

It was also evident that he had taken his training at Texas A&M and Officer Candidate School seriously. He was a teacher and a coach. He taught hand-to-hand combat, and I don't think any man in the company could have taken him down. He was always teaching. For instance, it was hot in the desert and men were running out of canteen water early in the day, so he taught us how to ration our water.

He was decisive. He knew what to do as a platoon leader and how to do it. I remember another night maneuver where we were going to be navigating by moonlight. We were given instructions as to how to proceed, which we implemented. It did not take long before he stopped the platoon, said that even though we were doing it "by the book," we were off track. He changed direction, which turned out to be the right decision. In platoon and company maneuvers, he knew what to.

He won our respect because he showed respect for us, and he won our allegiance because he was a leader. He was confident without being arrogant, which strengthened our loyalty to him. We knew that, though we were going into battle and there would be casualties, he would make good decisions and do his best to take care of us. The pattern he established in training was later born out in battle. He was not foolhardy; he was focused, weighed options when time permitted, and did not put any of us needlessly into harm's way. If a mission was particularly dangerous, he would lead it himself.

Soldiers want and deserve good leaders. Many books have been written about the subject. There are different styles of leadership. Most men instinctively sense the quality of leadership in another, and that engenders trust, confidence, and unit cohesion. Lieutenant Adkisson led in various ways, but mostly he led by example. Long before we left for Europe, he proved that he was a strong and capable leader. We would not hesitate to follow him. We were not disappointed.

**

Midway through our training, we got a new company commander, Emmett McCrary, who was a first lieutenant from Georgia. He was twenty-four years old, slim, with brown hair, and medium height. He took his job very seriously and left no doubt that he was in command. He was fair and levelheaded, but he had no illusions of being in a popularity contest. He could be demanding, tough, and fearless. He was no stranger to salty language, but he could also offer up a stirring prayer at the appropriate time. He could dress down an individual or a group of men in no uncertain terms when they made a mistake, then end with, "Things like that can get men killed." I think the men knew that, despite his abrasive manner, he ultimately had their safety and survival in mind, and they came to respect him as a leader. He and I had the same priorities and, though we had different styles of leadership, formed a close bond and learned to work together well.

I became good friends with another lieutenant, Tom Spoerer, a friendly, easy-going Pennsylvanian. One Friday night after we had spent a week in the field doing maneuvers, we got a day off and headed into the thriving metropolis of Yuma. We had been subsisting on K-rations during the entire week, and were hungry for a good hot meal. We found a restaurant, were seated, and both ordered the biggest steak on the menu, which tasted great. About the time we finished our steak, the waiter walked by carrying a half of a chicken to another customer. We both agreed that it looked pretty good, so we each ordered a half of a chicken to finish off our meal.

When we did get hot chow, it was good. We had a company mess sergeant, James Pedula, who had owned a delicatessen in Memphis before he joined the army. I don't know how he did it, but he was able to take bland ingredients and turn them into gourmet meals. The men loved his cooking. One of the best Christmas dinners I have ever had was the one prepared by Sergeant Pedula on Christmas day 1943. We had turkey and dressing and all of the trimmings, which was quite a treat, especially considering that we were in the desert.

As our time allocation for desert training wound down, the company got orders to take our rolling stock to Pomona, California, where it would be loaded onto trains to be shipped to various fourth-echelon shops to be rebuilt. The sand had taken its toll. Most of the men boarded trucks and headed to California. On their arrival, they worked in shifts, loading equipment for most of a twenty-four-hour day, and then got twenty-four hours off. I did not make the trip, however, because I was assigned the duty of training newly arrived recruits. I heard a few stories when the men got back, but I really didn't listen with much enthusiasm.

Upon their return, most of the division was trucked down to El Centro, California, where we boarded trains to head for Ft. Dix, New Jersey. While the troops headed to the East Coast, I took a few days of the leave I had earned and diverted to West Texas.

New Jersey

After a few days of soaking up home and family, my new bride and I said our good-byes and left Lubbock on the train bound for the East Coast. We had a stopover in Chicago, where I told Marie that this was a perfect opportunity to see my childhood buddy, Roy Williams, who was in the navy in training. We booked a room in a hotel and took a cab from the train station. We had quite a bit of baggage and, on being dropped off at our destination, I tipped the cabbie a dollar. He became very indignant about my lack of generosity and made somewhat of a scene until I came up with a few more dollars. We didn't spend a lot of time in cabs in West Texas, nor did people behave that way when they had a disagreement. It was embarrassing, but I shook it off and we had a great time with Roy.

We arrived in New Jersey with no place to live, but that turned out to be a minor issue. There were lists of people posted on the company bulletin board who rented out rooms to soldiers, which was common practice for people who lived near military bases during the war years. We rented a room right away, along with four other young officers and their wives, from Mrs. Anderson in Trenton, New Jersey, which allowed us to spend a few months together as a married couple before I shipped out.

We had not been in Fort Dix long when we were awakened at 4:00 one morning by the sound of sirens going off all over the city. We did not know what was going on or what it meant until someone told us that the invasion of Europe had begun. It was June 6, 1944.

We had some form of training almost every day, which kept me busy. One day the company commander directed me to set up the rifle range for company rifle grenade qualification. Rifle grenades enabled an infantryman to have at least some defense against armor (tanks), and could be used as antipersonnel weapons as well. A two-piece adapter was fitted over the end of the barrel of a standard M1 rifle and a grenade was loaded into the adapter. The shooter inserted a special blank shell into the chamber, pulled the pin on the grenade, and fired. The grenade did not arm until it left the adapter. I went to the range and was just about set up when a private pulled up in a jeep and informed me that the training had been expanded to include the whole battalion. Then, within a short time, the training was expanded further to include the entire regiment. I made changes accordingly. To get ready, I had fired a number of practice rounds and determined that the best way to get an accurate shot on the target was to elevate the barrel and use the stacking swivel as a guide, rather than the gun sight. The stacking swivel on an M1 is a small piece of metal located on the bottom of the rifle about six inches from the end of the barrel. It is held in place by a pin, which allows it to swivel fore and aft. It also has a small hook on each side. By interlocking the hooks, three rifles could be stacked together, with rifle butts on the ground and barrels pointing skyward.

The first man to take a turn on the firing range was the regimental commander, Colonel Donald Cameron, a stocky officer with a broad face who exuded quiet confidence and no-nonsense leadership. An experienced career army man now in his mid-forties, he had served in World War I in the enlisted ranks, and had earned promotions in the years between the wars. The gap between a career army colonel commanding a regiment and a green second lieutenant leading a platoon covered quite a span, so this was one of my few direct encounters with the man.

He fired the weapon, looked at me, and said, "Lieutenant, I did exactly what you said, and I didn't hit the target." I wasn't quite sure how to respond, but he let it go at that and did not say anything more about it. This experience indicated to me that he wasn't petty and kept things in perspective, an assessment that proved to be accurate in the months to come.

Following the grenade training, I was tasked with taking a group of men in the company out to conduct bazooka training, which required a number of demonstration shots. The bazooka was a dirty weapon to fire. Standard procedure was to fire from a kneeling or prone position, so the firing area of the range was covered with sand. The rocket was 2.36 inches (60mm) in diameter, and, as it left the barrel, it would blow sand in your face and leave small black burn marks. On the first day of training, I went directly home from the range. When I walked in the door, Marie looked at me and said, "What in the world happened to you?" I didn't realize it, but my face was covered with black sand burns. They were all gone within a couple of days.

At one point during our stay, I found out that I had been "volunteered" to take an advanced infantry test, along with several other lieutenants in the regiment. We did two exercises on day one. The first exercise was a nine-mile hike that had to be completed in two hours, which meant that we had to run a good portion of the distance. It took some effort, but I made the hike with a few minutes to spare. We took a rest break and reported for our second exercise. Our next assignment was to run two hundred yards with a gas mask on, which just about ripped my lungs out. That was a miserable experience—worse than the nine-mile hike by an order of magnitude. The next day, we had to cover twenty-five miles in eight hours with full combat gear, but by that time, I was in such good physical condition that it was not overly stressful.

By the time we were ready to leave Ft. Dix, I weighed in at a solid one hundred and eighty pounds, and was in the best shape of my life. As well, I had received just about all of the training that was available to a young lieutenant in the army. We were as ready as it was possible to be, both individually and as a unit, but I soon found out that no amount of training can fully prepare a man for actual combat.

Not long before we shipped out, I was able to obtain a weekend pass and took Marie to Radio City Music Hall to see the Rockettes. We spent the night in a hotel in New York after the performance and it was quite a treat. A few years before, I would never have believed that I would be in New York City, much less at Radio City Music Hall, being entertained by a world-famous group. The place was very ornate and the furnishings and lighting were extravagant. The girls lived up to their reputation and put on quite a show.

I was as committed as anyone to doing my part in the war, but I did not harbor any premonitions of death. My resolve to return home in one piece was further strengthened by my wife's announcement just before we shipped out that she was "pretty sure" she was pregnant.

Shipping Out

The 80th Infantry Division shipped out on July 1, 1944, aboard the *Queen Mary*. The former luxury liner had been converted into a troop transport with hardly a single square inch wasted. We were packed in like sardines. The massive ship could make 30 knots, a speed that no convoy could match, so we traveled alone. After we got underway, the ship's captain announced over the public address system that there were seventeen thousand troops and eight hundred crew members on board. Our destination was Glasgow, Scotland, and travel time would be approximately seven days. All hands were to stay away from the railings, as there would be no turning the ship around in the event of a man overboard. Our main danger during the voyage was German submarines, so we would be following a zigzag course to avoid torpedoes. He explained that the elapsed time between being sighted by a submarine, its launching of a torpedo, and impact was eight minutes. Therefore, the ship would be changing course every seven minutes.

The ship was so full that half of the men in our company slept on deck. The officers stayed in separate quarters, but we were no less cramped than the enlisted men. I stayed in a twenty-foot by twenty-foot stateroom with seventeen other second lieutenants. We rotated guard duty and I had the 4 a.m. to 7 a.m. shift. Other than routine oversight, our main responsibility as company-grade officers was to make sure that the troops made it to chow and back through a maze of passageways. The rule was that the starboard side was for forward movement and port was for movement aft. We were told that a wrong turn could result in as much as an eight-hour delay due to the number of men who had to be fed, so I went on board three days prior to departure to make sure I had the route down pat. We ate two meals a day. The chow was adequate, but there never seemed to be enough of it.

We were all ground pounders and, except for a few, this was our first time at sea. That meant that a lot of men were seasick the entire journey. In spite of the warning to stay away from the railings, there were times that there was hardly any room for another soldier to crowd in to throw up over the side.

The trip was utterly boring: nothing to do and nowhere to go. Card games abounded. We did, however, have a couple of incidents that brought us to full alert, if only for a few moments. When we had been at sea for a few days, my company was in the chow line for our first of two daily meals when, all of a sudden, we heard the sound of the antiaircraft guns firing. Our first thought was that we were under attack. There was no place to run and hide, so everyone looked around nervously, waiting for who-knew-what. The word was soon passed that the crew was making sure the guns worked properly and there was nothing to worry about. It would have been nice if one of the ship's officers had announced the practice shoot beforehand.

The next day, we were minding our own business when the air raid alarm sounded and we all had to get below decks. It turned out to be a false alarm. We had radio silence throughout the trip, so a British plane had flown out to signal the ship with a blinking light. From then on, the Brits sent a plane out every morning to circle the ship as a crewman blinked Morse code signals to the ship. Card games notwithstanding, the mood aboard ship was serious; there was not much joking around or horseplay. We knew that we were headed into combat, that not all of us were coming back.

When we arrived in Glasgow, the ship's draft was too deep to allow us to dock, so we offloaded into small landing craft. We were loaded down with full packs and rifles, and we climbed down cargo nets to board the landing vessels, a maneuver that was a bit tricky as the landing boats bobbed up and down. When we pulled into the dock, we were greeted by a Scottish band decked out in kilts, playing military marches with bagpipes. It was now July 1944.

After our arrival in Scotland we were transported to Aston-Keynes in England to await transport to France. Our living quarters consisted of tents set up on what was formerly a golf course.

We were kept occupied with more training, including night hikes, which were fairly short because Scotland is so far north that the nights were only a few hours long at this time of year. I shared a tent with Tom Spoerer, who had acquired a bicycle. I usually woke up before he did and we were not too far from the mess tent, so I would often "borrow" his bike to go get some breakfast. He would wake up, get ready, and realize that I had taken his bike. I could hear him all the way in the mess tent hollering, "Goddamn you, Adkisson, you stole my bike again." He would walk over to get some chow, and after we were done eating, I would ride back on the handlebars while he pedaled. We were both assigned to Able Company, so we began our combat tours together. Unfortunately, we did not finish together.

Chapter 5
In the Theatre
August 6, 1944–September 3, 1944

On August 6, D-Day plus 60, our regiment disembarked on Utah Beach without incident. We were brought across the English Channel on small troop transports, taken ashore via landing craft, and dropped off in three feet of water. Able Company had a full complement of troops: one captain, three first lieutenants, two second lieutenants, and 188 enlisted men. The 80th Division was assigned to the XX Corps, part of the Third Army, which meant we were under Lieutenant General George Patton's command.

We finished unloading at 0230 hours, marched a few miles in our soggy boots, and were then carried in trucks to the village of Coigny, France, northwest of St. Lo, where we spent the rest of our first full night on the Continent in an apple orchard. Each soldier was packing a cumbersome load of gear, so our first order of business the next day was to get rid of our gas masks. The Germans were not engaging in any form of chemical warfare, so we were instructed to throw all of our gas masks in a pile, thus lightening our load slightly. The masks were the first of numerous items we discarded as the days and miles of marching went by.

All of our vehicles were marked by division, regiment, and battalion. The motor pool guys covered the markings with mud to keep our arrival as covert as possible, but it apparently did not work very well. Someone in our company had acquired a small radio, and that night we heard the voice of Axis Sally over the airwaves, welcoming the 80th Division to Continental Europe.

The Situation
During the two months between D-Day and the day we landed, the U.S. Army had been moving men and material into northwestern France. Although our troops met with fierce

31

resistance from the Germans fighting through the hedgerow country of Normandy, within three weeks of D-Day, our most forward positions were about twenty miles inland. In spite of a lack of ports, by July 1 almost a million men, more than a half-million tons of supplies, and 177,000 vehicles had been landed.

The Allied strategic plan was to move south into Brittany and secure additional ports to facilitate the establishment of air and supply bases in northern France from the coast eastward to the Seine River. From there, we would advance in line into Germany. This would be a joint effort with General Omar Bradley commanding American troops and General Bernard Montgomery leading the British troops, along with the First Canadian Army and some Polish units. The 80th Division was given the assignment of moving south towards Brittany.

General Patton believed that rapid movement, versus deliberate movement with cautious attention to flanks, reduced the chance of casualties, so our push to the south was going to be simple and fast. As we launched southward, the Germans, in an effort to cut off the Allied advance toward Brittany, committed tens of thousands of troops on August 7 to a large-scale attack westward from Mortain. If their plan worked, they would be able to slice through the Third Army lines, isolate us from all support, and thrash us. Nevertheless, in a real-life chess game, their move opened the door for a devastating countermove.

As the Germans made their play, the Allied generals quickly recognized that they were being given a golden opportunity. If they acted quickly, rather than being cut off by Hitler's forces, they would be able to turn the tables and entrap the German army in the area of Argentan. General Bradley was quoted as saying, "This is an opportunity that comes to a commander not more than once in a century. We are about to destroy an entire hostile army." The situation dictated a change in strategy. The U.S. Third Army was ordered to abandon the southward march, join up with Lieutenant General Courtney Hodges's U.S. First Army, and proceed at once to the area of Argentan. British and Canadian forces to the north moved toward Falaise as U.S. troops wheeled up from the south to encircle the German army and place it in the jaws of a military vise roughly halfway between St. Lo and Paris. The 80th Division's first combat assignment was to hem in the German army from the south, move into Argentan, and attack. We would remain primarily under the control of the XX Corps during this period of action.

The Allied plan worked almost to perfection. The western German army, under the command of Field Marshall Günther von Kluge, was soon boxed in on three sides. The Germans were thus cut off from their supply lines following several days of heavy Allied aerial bombardment, and they knew they had no chance of success in battle. Their only viable option was to escape eastward through a ten-mile span between the cities of Falaise, to the north, and Argentan, to the south, referred to as the Argentan–Falaise gap. On being briefed, Hitler issued orders to launch an offensive. He saw this as an opportunity to "push the Allies back to the sea." The German field commanders knew that they were faced with overwhelming odds and the Führer's perception of things was utterly unrealistic. Nonetheless, in obedience to Hitler's orders, they spent several days reorganizing and trying to work out a battle plan, all while being pummeled by Allied air, artillery, and ground troops. After what Hitler perceived as a sluggish response to his orders, von Kluge was relieved of duty and ordered to return to Berlin. He was replaced by Field Marshal Walter Model who quickly assessed the situation and convinced Hitler that, unless they were to be supplied with massive reinforcements, they needed to retreat to the east. Hitler compromised and approved a retreat, but it was to be spearheaded by an attack to widen the Argentan–Falaise gap.

Von Kluge dispatched a letter to Hitler imploring him to end the war and spare the country, then on the way to Berlin, in full expectation that he would be the scapegoat for the impending failure of the Mortain attack, ended his life with a cyanide tablet.

Moving In

At the company and platoon level, we were never fully apprised of, nor were we particularly interested in, the overall strategy of the Allies or the U.S. Army. Our focus was always on the mission of the day. We did not know at the time that we were about to be a part of one of the major victories in the European Theatre of Operations (ETO).

After a couple of days in Coigny, we traveled sixty miles by truck to a town just south of Avranches, a port city. As we traveled, I got my first sobering glimpse of what lay ahead when we were met by an oncoming jeep. We were traveling by truck, a 6x6 with a canvas cover. I was standing up front, leaning on the roof of the truck, looking out from under the cover, curious as to what kind of country we were moving into. The jeep was carrying a stretcher with a wounded soldier strapped in place. As I watched them go by, I saw that his face was pasty white and the lower part of his shirt was soaked with blood. It was my first connection to the cold-hearted consequences of war; no more training films or men "wounded" in a field exercise hopping back to their feet afterwards and heading to the chow line.

The following night, we moved by truck southwest another seventy miles to Vaiges, a town on the Laval–LeMans highway, about sixty miles south of Argentan. It was during this trip that I issued my first order as a platoon leader to prepare to engage the enemy in a combat zone.

Our battalion's assignment was to proceed to a bridge that had been taken by another outfit and defend it against counterattack. We were in a convoy of trucks, "blacked out," meaning the front and rear lights were covered except for several horizontal slits to allow for a small amount of illumination. Our battalion commander, Lieutenant Colonel Frank Norman, and the battalion operations officer were in a jeep ahead of the convoy. My platoon was in the first two trucks. After traveling a short distance, the operations officer, Willis King, tapped the CO on the shoulder and said, "Sir, we don't know exactly where we are. There is no one in front of us, and we don't know where the enemy is."

The colonel abruptly stopped the convoy and told the ops officer to have me unload my men and advance about a hundred yards ahead of the convoy to see what was in front of us. I remember, with great clarity, dismounting from the trucks and forming up, getting ready to move out in the dark. I issued the order, "Lock and load." This was the real deal. I still get goose bumps when I think about it.

As it turned out, the Germans had mounted a weak counterattack but had been repulsed by another unit. We made contact with our forces and things remained quiet. We didn't see any action that night, but we did not have to wait long.

By August 10, the 80th Division was tasked specifically with securing and holding the road from Laval east to Le Mans, which was an important supply route. Hence our assignment and transport to the town of Vaiges. From there, we moved northwest from village to village, zigzagging through small towns such as Sille-le-Guillaime, Segrie, and Villaines-la-Juhel, where we conducted clearing operations. There were occasional German stragglers, but very few. The goal was to make it to Argentan to help close the gap and trap the German forces. Though we accomplished little in terms of weakening the enemy, we became more accustomed to life as infantrymen at war in the U.S. Army.

Fighting Cooks and Foxholes

The events that take place in a war zone are often laced with irony. An effort by the enemy to inflict suffering can end up supplying comic relief, especially in retrospect. We had a couple of men who had not taken our training in Yuma very seriously. They especially did not like digging foxholes. I had to stay on them constantly. They finally learned their lesson one day soon after we began our move toward Argentan, when we had a visit from a German fighter plane.

We had stopped to bivouac in some woods when we heard the sound of an approaching airplane. The engine noise quickly grew louder, indicating that he was approaching our position at a low altitude. Everyone looked up as he came in over the treetops. No sooner had we made out the German crosses on the underside of his wings than he released a bomb. It landed near the kitchen, a hundred yards to our rear, but caused no damage or casualties. The cooks, in a rare show of defiance, took it on themselves to retaliate. The mess trucks had a ring-mounted .50-caliber machine gun on a frame above the truck bed. One of the cooks was in the mess truck when the plane flew over and immediately he manned the gun, swung it around in the direction of the plane, and fired a long burst. Apparently, the German pilot did not appreciate this gesture. He circled back for another pass. This time he flew even lower and made a long strafing run. Again, no one was hit. As he flew off into the distance, things got very quiet. Within a few seconds, I heard the sound of someone digging furiously. It was my two wayward trainees. "I thought you guys didn't believe in digging foxholes," I said.

"No use being a damned fool all of your life," one of them replied. I didn't have to say any more to them about digging foxholes.

**

A few days later, when we had stopped to take a break during a march, we found ourselves spectators to a tank battle. Someone spotted a couple of German tanks coming around a steep hill about a half mile away from us. They were on a narrow road that had been graded out of the hillside. On an opposite hill, three of our tanks were in defilade, with just their turrets exposed. As we sat in the cool shade of some trees, sipping from our canteens, we watched the two German tanks come around the corner. Our tanks took aim and fired off a volley. The Germans returned fire. With each round fired, flames belched out of the barrels, followed by the impact at the other end. Not unlike a deadly tennis match, each group took turns firing. After about ten minutes, one of our tanks hit the track of the lead German tank, which stopped its progress and left it stranded. The second tank backed around the bend, but we couldn't see what happened to the crew of the lead tank. We had not yet experienced the fury of tank fire, so the episode smacked of being mildly entertaining. Our perspective would soon change.

Closing the Gap

The Germans had begun their retreat through the Argentan–Falaise gap on August 16, traveling under the cover of darkness as much as possible. By August 18, our regiment was stationed just outside of Argentan. The 318th Infantry Regiment was assigned the mission of taking the town. They were to bypass the town to the east and attack from the northeast. We were in division reserve.

The enemy was well dug in and prepared. After most of a day of fierce fighting, the 318th had to pull back, having taken heavy casualties. The following day, we received notice that we would be joining our sister regiment in the next attempt to take the town. It would be our first real test in battle as a unit.

Seven battalions of artillery, two from the 80th Division and five from XII Corps, would be supporting the attack. Again, there was fierce fighting led by the 318th Infantry and parts of our regiment.

Able Company, 1st Battalion, 317th Infantry, moved out of our bivouac area at midnight, August 19. It was assigned to take the high ground east of the city, but we did not immediately go into the attack. We jumped off at 0700 hours on August 20.

We hadn't gone very far before we began to take small arms fire from a hedgerow to our front. (Fields in the Normandy area were bordered by hedgerows rather than fences, which provided natural cover for both sides.) We took cover in an opposing hedgerow, returned fire, and called up armor for support. One of our tanks pulled up and stopped a few yards away from where my platoon sergeant, Johnny Fabrizio, and I had taken cover. A German machine gun opened fire, but it had no effect on the tank's thick armor. Hearing the bullets ricocheting off of turret, I turned to my sergeant and said, "Johnny, if you've got to fight a war, that just might be the way to do it." At about that time, a German antitank round struck our tank at the base of the turret and blew it off. It tumbled over the back of the tank, taking the top half of the tank commander with it. As the tank caught on fire, one of my men rescued the driver and saved his life. I decided that I would take my chances on the ground, where I could duck. This was my introduction to combat.

We continued our attack on the Germans and drove them out of the hedgerow. They retreated across an open area and disappeared behind another hedgerow. We pursued them across the open area while receiving minimal return fire. We were moving forward across the open area when we came up on an abandoned enemy ammunition dump.

As we were surveying our find, we saw a German tank approaching from our front. It was apparent that his goal was to get to the dump as well. No wonder the foot soldiers were not firing back. They were going to let the tank take care of us. It came toward us, machine guns firing. We were caught by surprise and immediately took cover, which was scarce. Within a few seconds, I

37

realized that my instincts may not have served me well; I had taken cover behind a live 8-inch artillery round. The German tank made a right turn, then reversed field, and began to drive away from our platoon. As I was getting my men to move forward, Lieutenant Colonel Norman ran past me, heading for the rear. He shouted, "I am going back to get the TDs!"—meaning tank destroyers. This was puzzling behavior but I had my hands full and the colonel could do whatever he wanted.

The tank disappeared from view, so we moved forward past the ammo dump—until we again heard the sound of an engine. The tank was returning. I decided that we needed to get rid of this guy. I knew that we had a bazooka with us, so I called for it to be brought forward for a shot and yelled out to my platoon, "Which of you men have had bazooka training?" Silence. (I had given many of them bazooka training at Ft. Dix.) I grabbed the bazooka and told my runner, Pfc Elmer Roberts "Come on, Roberts, let's get him."

I got into position, took aim, and fired at the track on one side of the tank, but I missed high. The tank moved away from the area for a few moments, which allowed us to move further ahead such that the entire platoon was past the road the tank had been traveling on. It then came back across, passing behind the platoon. I wasn't sure what this guy's objective was, and I don't think he knew either. He seemed to be confused, but having an enemy tank drive around your platoon area can be quite menacing, whether the driver knows what he is doing or not. One of my men, Henry Karvonen, had a rifle grenade. Hank was a big Swede from Michigan with keen eyesight, hearing, and smell, all of which would come into play as time went on. He also proved from the outset to be very brave. I called him forward and gave him instructions, "Hank, wait until he goes past us and fire a grenade into the engine vent plate in the back as he goes by." He did just as I told him and got a direct hit on the vent plate. The tank burst into flames and ground to a halt. The German crewmen bailed out and surrendered to us. I recommended Karvonen for a Bronze Star Medal for his actions that day, and it was approved.

In the meantime, while the tank was maneuvering, one of my troops ran for cover and jumped into an artillery crater he had seen from a distance. There was dust and smoke in the air. It was a deep crater, so he could not see that seven German soldiers had already taken cover there. Before he could react, they all threw up their hands and surrendered. He later confided to me that they only beat him by a second, because he was just as startled as they were and he was about to throw up his hands in surrender. So, this private first class, on his first day of combat, captured of a small cadre of German soldiers.

The Germans retreated en masse through the ever-tightening gap during the night of August 19–20, fighting their way out while leaving a contingent of troops to cover their withdrawal, which they did quite effectively. Though the Germans tried to destroy equipment they were leaving behind, some of it was still serviceable and it was up to us to make sure anything of consequence was destroyed.

The day after our tank encounter, one of our patrols reported that a German tank was a short distance from our front, abandoned when it had run out of fuel. The colonel instructed me to take a squad to disarm the tank and blow it up. We went to the site, where I told a few of my men set up a perimeter to keep an eye out while I got two men to help me disarm the tank. The Germans were notorious for leaving booby-trapped equipment behind when they left an area, so I carefully looked everything over before I crawled into the tank, then I checked the inside before touching anything. I stationed a man next to the hatch so I could pass the ammo to him. I carefully lifted out the first round and handed it over, followed by another, and another, until we were done. We laid out the ammunition a safe distance from the tank. If we set it on fire with the 88mm rounds inside, we would no doubt start our own little artillery barrage, and there was no telling what direction the rounds would go or when they would go off. I had one of my bazooka men use the tank for target practice. After a couple of rounds, the tank was in flames. We returned to our company area, where we had a surprise waiting for us.

Just as we returned to the area from destroying the tank, a German major came out of a wooded area carrying a white flag. The company held fire and waited. The Germans were surrendering in droves at this point, but we had not yet taken more than a few prisoners. This major was a battalion commander who had realized that he was surrounded and had no chance of escape.

He surrendered what remained of his unit, which consisted of three hundred men and officers. They were bedraggled and hungry, so we put them under temporary guard and issued some K-rations.

The prisoners had to be taken to the nearest POW camp. Lieutenant Colonel Norman told me to take several men and escort these prisoners to a prisoner-of-war (POW) camp that was located seven kilometers away. We left on foot at about 1400 hours. On arrival at the destination we had been given, we were informed that the camp had been moved seven kilometers to the north, so we marched some more. When we got to the second site, we were told that the camp had just been relocated seven kilometers to the west. This was getting old. We finally found the camp at 2:00 in the morning. After turning the Germans over to the camp commander, we boarded a truck and were taken back to our company, where we arrived just before daybreak.

The last Germans escaped through the Falaise Gap on the night of August 20. The battle ended and things became calm. There was never a conclusive count of the German casualties or prisoners, but the estimates were ten thousand dead and fifty thousand captured.

The 80th Division's job from this point to the end of the war was to push the Germans to the east, back to their homeland, taking back territory they had occupied, killing and capturing as many as possible as we went. Our first battle-our baptism in war-was a battle of major historical significance.

Regrouping After the Breakout

One of my first—and unanticipated—impressions as we traveled to Argentan and beyond was the smell of rotting flesh, both human and animal. The Germans used horses to pull artillery pieces and other equipment, so there were scores of bloated horse carcasses lying on their sides along the roads with all four limbs stiffened out, along with an occasional German soldier's corpse. The stench was horrible, a smell that you never forget, especially the smell of rotting human flesh. There was also a seemingly endless trail of destroyed and abandoned equipment along the roads—artillery pieces, trucks, rifles, pistols, kitchen equipment, all the way down to mess kits. The Germans were paying a high price for starting the war.

By now we had been in combat for two weeks, enough time for each man's true colors and abilities—or lack thereof—to show. We had one man in our company who spoke German. He had been sort of a goof-off during our Stateside training and was exempt from strenuous duty due to a problem with one of his testicles, which descended if he overexerted himself. He insisted that the condition gave him a lot of pain, and the doctors couldn't refute his claim. The result was that, during most of our company's training and maneuvers, he was assigned to KP and other headquarters duties. Nevertheless, when we got into combat, he surprised everyone by putting his German-speaking ability to good use. On several occasions, when we were able to get close enough to the enemy to communicate verbally, he talked them into laying down their arms and surrendering. He was responsible for the surrender of quite a few German soldiers and was eventually commissioned as a second lieutenant.

We also had one man in our company who had a very keen sense of smell. We all employed this sense at one time or another. When we entered a house that had been occupied by German soldiers, we could detect a distinct odor. Inasmuch as we all went weeks without bathing or changing clothes, we emanated a distinct odor of our own. But this man was unique. Like a good hunting dog, if the Germans were upwind, he could smell them. One night, when it was pitch black, he told his platoon leader that he could smell Germans and pointed out the direction of the odor. An automatic weapon was brought up and the area was sprayed with bullets. Sure enough, several dead German soldiers were found in the firing zone the next morning.

Moving East

We bivouacked near a small river for a few days while replacement troops were brought in along with supplies and equipment. Since we had arrived in France, we had barely had an opportunity to wash our faces, let alone clean or change clothes. The river offered an opportunity to feel clean again, so we went down to the bank, stripped off our clothes, and proceeded to take baths. We were all scrubbing merrily away when I heard someone say, "Look." We all looked up and saw a bridge about fifty yards away lined with men, women, and children watching us and laughing. Spectators or not, it still felt good to be clean. We didn't know it at the time, but this would be the last bath we would take for many weeks.

**

The strategic situation at this point was that the Germans were retreating eastward across northern France with the Allies in close pursuit. As they retreated, they left small rear-guard groups in abandoned towns or villages to disrupt our advance. We traveled from village to village, marching if the distance was less than fifteen miles or so, on trucks if it was longer. As we advanced, the various units leap-frogged. The lead unit entering a village conducted the clearing action, after which it would hold up and allow the units behind it to pass through and lead the way to the next village. We set up a perimeter every night, stationed outposts, and, if we occupied ground outside the village, usually dug foxholes.

We saw civilians, and though there were no welcoming celebrations such as the ones shown in the newsreels of American troops entering Paris, the villagers often expressed their appreciation in a more subdued way. Sometimes, as we approached a village, the church bells began to ring. Some of our men initially thought the locals were warning the Germans, but we soon realized that it was their way of celebrating their liberation. They kept mostly to themselves, and their visibility was dependent on the level of enemy presence. If, on our arrival, people came out to meet us, we knew there were no Germans nearby. On the other hand, if we entered a village and it was quiet, with no civilian activity, we could bet that the enemy was in the area—either in the village proper, or just outside. The civilians knew how to make themselves scarce. We took our cues from them as to how to proceed in our house-to-house searches, because they could be trusted to inform us if a particular house or building was occupied.

We quickly became adept at moving through villages and searching houses and buildings. If we had any suspicion that a building was occupied, we opened or knocked down a door and threw in a hand grenade, which was usually pretty effective at flushing out bad guys. It didn't take long before the contents of an empty house became fair game, at least in the case of food or an occasional libation. Potatoes and canned goods were stored in cellars; meat, especially ham, was often hung inside the chimney. Eggs could be anywhere inside or outside.

The handiest way to carry fruit or eggs was to take your steel helmet off and load it up, leaving the plastic helmet liner on your head. This worked fine if the enemy left us alone.

One day, as we moved through a small village, we were told that we would be staying in it overnight. That gave the men enough time to catch some chickens and gather up some eggs. Then, before the scavengers could convert their spoils into a meal, orders were abruptly changed and we were told to move out. Several of the men held out for an opportunity to enjoy the fresh eggs that they were carrying in their helmets as we started single-file down a road. Their hopes came to an abrupt end when the Germans lobbed an artillery shell at us. Without thinking, they instinctively slammed their helmets on and hit the deck. Any chicken in captivity was immediately given its freedom and all the eggs were instantly scrambled. Nobody was hurt, but the bill of fare for the evening was cancelled.

Learning to Travel

As the month of August 1944 drew to a close, we had survived one significant battle and a few skirmishes while sustaining very few casualties. When we first entered France, we brought full packs, but as we traveled, we gradually streamlined our load. In addition to our M1 rifles, and in a few cases, carbines, we had a utility belt with a canteen and canvas packets that carried clips or magazines of ammunition. We started off with hand grenades, but found that we seldom used them, so each squad had a couple of men who carried them while the rest did not. We also did not carry bayonets, though they were available to us. Each man found a place to keep a spoon and a razor. A couple of men in a squad carried soap, which was passed around when we had a chance to clean up a little. We did not carry mess kits, because the silverware inside rattled. The metal mess kits were kept with the company kitchen crew. We had been issued sleeping bags when we entered

France, but no one dared to crawl into a sleeping bag and zip it up, so they quickly disappeared. I don't know what happened to them.

Communications

We never knew for sure if the Germans were listening to our wireless radio conversations; we assumed that they could hear everything. We used a sort of low-grade code to prevent disclosing troop strength or disposition. So, unless we were in the heat of battle, if we needed a medic and his name was Corporal Jones, we would say, "I would sure like to see Corporal Jones." If we needed ammunition and the person to contact was named Smith, we might say, "How is Sergeant Smith doing? I would sure like to see him." Though we knew the Germans could not monitor land-line communication, out of habit, we followed the same practice when talking on the phone.

Maps and Patrols

Our focus at the company and platoon level had not changed. We were only vaguely focused on the big picture and primarily occupied with what lay directly in front of us. We had down time, but we were seldom stationary for long. If we were not moving to another village, we were digging in or sending out patrols for the purpose of seeing what was in front of us. The other, less pleasant, purpose of patrols was to draw enemy fire, and thereby flush out enemy locations. Patrols were usually squad-size or smaller. As a platoon commander, I led most of our patrols, regardless of the number of men going out.

Most patrols ended up being uneventful, which was fine with us, but we seldom knew what we would run into and never relaxed or took anything for granted. The tension was diminished somewhat if the route offered good cover and concealment.

Any foray across an open field or a low-lying area was hazardous, to say the least, so we often took major detours to stay in a tree line and minimize the threat of being spotted. Of course, the Germans did the same thing, so both sides risked being ambushed or captured no matter how much care went into planning the patrol. We used maps and visual recon to determine patrol routes. We did not depend on something colorful made up by a map company, but rather on some pretty sophisticated technology for the day. I don't know how it was done, but every night, weather permitting, photo-reconnaissance planes flew over the lines and took pictures, which formed the basis for area maps that would be in the hands of company commanders by the next morning. The maps showed the terrain and villages in our area, which was a great help in deciding on patrol routes and maneuvers.

If we were going on a patrol or moving as a company, sometimes the company commander would call the platoon commanders in to review maps. At other times, we were simply given orders and moved out. Most patrol orders had an obvious purpose, but occasionally a commander would give an order that defied common sense. I had one company commander who approached me late one afternoon and said, "Gid, send out a patrol." And then he walked away. I thought about it for a few minutes and called Sergeant Karvonen over.

"Hank, do you see that tree about fifty yards away?"

"Yes, sir."

"Take a couple of men to the tree and back, and report to me what you find."

He did as he was told, which meant that I did as I was told. The CO never followed up.

We occasionally sent out a motorized patrol, which created every bit as much tension as a foot patrol. One time we took three jeeps about four miles through a wooded area. There were four people in each jeep, and every man was assigned a sector to scan. At the end of our patrol route was a small village. When we got there, the villagers were distraught. They said the Germans had left about ten minutes prior to our arrival, but before leaving they had shot and killed an old man for unknown reasons and covered him with a piece of sheet metal. We were sympathetic, but there was nothing we could do at this point. We reported back to our unit.

Germans In Retreat

We crossed many streams and not a few rivers as we moved across Europe. The Germans destroyed as many bridges as they could during their retreat, so our method for crossing these natural landmarks varied. If a stream was shallow enough to permit, we waded across. If we had to cross a river too deep to ford, we depended on the combat engineers to supply boats or ferries, or set up pontoon bridges. Pontoon bridges with tracks laid across them were used to move vehicles.

Though they were moving back towards the Motherland and therefore on the defensive, the Germans did what they could to inflict pain and suffering on us as they went. They sometimes left a small contingent of men on an easy-to-defend piece of real estate to harass us with small arms fire. They also registered artillery on road intersections, river crossings, or other key terrain spots, then waited for us to move into the target area, at which time they dropped artillery on us. Private Justin Baca, from New Mexico, found out firsthand how accurate the artillery could be one day just prior to our crossing a small river. He was bringing up a load of ammunition from battalion supply in one of the company jeeps, accompanied by another private known as "Shorty." Traveling through a heavily wooded area, they were well concealed most of the way, but they eventually had to drive across an open area. As soon as they popped out into the open, an artillery round landed behind them. A few seconds later, another round landed in front of them.

"GET OUT!" shouted Baca. Without taking the jeep out of gear, they both rolled out and into ditches on either side of the road. The next round was a direct hit on the jeep, making for a spectacular explosion. They both escaped injury.

The Germans also deployed snipers from time to time. Their most sinister weapons however, were mines and booby traps. If we were going to travel down a road, we tried to have the engineers sweep the road first and clear it of mines.

To Eastern France

On August 26, the 80th Division reverted to the control of the XII Corps, commanded by Major General Manton Eddy. General Eddy reported to Lieutenant General George Patton, commander of the Third Army.

The long-range Allied plan at the corps level was for XII and XX corps to move east-northeast, form a unified front, and advance into western Germany, especially the Ruhr River Valley, which was a prominent industrial area supplying the war effort. XX Corps was to move north and then east through Liege, Belgium. XII Corps would move through Metz, France, and swing north. Also, II Corps would come on line for this advance. Our division was to be a part of the group moving through Metz. General Eddy had two primary phase lines to contend with before turning north: the Seine River, and the Rhine River. The Rhine was a major symbolic landmark for the Germans, so our crossing would be a blow to the morale of the German hierarchy.

On August 27, our division more or less shifted gears and traveled east two hundred fifty miles by truck. Our regiment occupied a village called La Pavillion. The next day, we traveled another sixty miles to Ecury sur Coole. From there, we crossed several rivers in succession: the Seine, Aube, Marne, and Meuse. In every case, the bridges were blown and we crossed on pontoons. There was light resistance at several of the crossings, but our advance was generally unopposed, aided in part by French Forces of the Interior (FFI), who were effectively taking out snipers and small German forces in our path.

We would certainly have had a major battle at the Meuse but for a fortunate bit of timing by our artillery observers. Before committing 80th Division troops to the crossing, a small team from division artillery climbed atop Mont Sec, which overlooks the entire Meuse Valley, to pick potential target coordinates for support as the infantry moved forward. The team took cover behind a monument dedicated to the 80th Division's participation in the St. Mihiel Campaign of World War I. They did a double-take at what they saw as they looked down into the valley. Just on the other side of the river were hundreds of German soldiers detraining, forming into platoons and companies, and preparing to set up a defense against the Allied river crossing. Noting and then rechecking map coordinates, the team called in a barrage of artillery on the unsuspecting soldiers from almost every piece of artillery in the 80th Division. It was a turkey shoot; the Germans never knew what hit them. The fortunate consequence of this event was that the division met virtually no resistance while crossing the river, which we accomplished on September 1.

Our regiment crossed the Meuse at Sampigny, a suburb of Commercy, the key town in the area. After regrouping, Able

Company's first assignment was to move one mile east to the town of Boncourt, where the Germans welcomed us with a lively fire fight that lasted an hour and a half. We suffered a couple of minor casualties and took a hundred prisoners.

After the crossing was completed and the bridgehead was firmly established, patrols from various companies were sent out through small towns in the direction of Pont-à-Mousson, a medium-size town on the west bank of the Moselle River, our next major objective. Pont-à-Mousson was twenty-four miles northeast of Commercy and it was to be the center of the regimental assembly area for our crossing of the river. Minor resistance was encountered as the patrols, followed by companies and battalions, made their way to the Moselle over a three-day period. We normally would have moved much faster, but rumor had it that the Third Army was running low on fuel. The Germans had created some mayhem before withdrawing across the river by burning the village of Martincourt to the ground and killing fifteen civilians. They also burned Nettancourt and Laheycourt.

Chapter 6
The Moselle River and Bloody Knob
September 3, 1944–September 20, 1944

In preparation for the crossing of the Moselle, our regimental reconnaissance platoon, led by Major Hayes, the regimental intelligence officer, was sent out ahead of the division on September 3 to conduct a visual recon of the enemy disposition beyond the river. Maintaining as much stealth as possible, they picked out observation posts on the west bank, got out the binoculars, and began a scan of the opposing terrain. They saw that the bridge had been blown and observed troop movement in a number of locations. Even though they were a small party, they were spotted and came under small arms and artillery fire. We had disrupted whatever German plan was in place at the Meuse, but our four-day delay in moving to the Moselle was handing them plenty of time to set up for a brutal welcome when we were ready to cross.

Our company also sent a platoon to undertake a physical recon of potential crossing points. Major Hayes had made his observations ahead of the patrol elements approaching the river and was able to warn them before they arrived. They came under fire and quickly took cover as Hayes's group moved to higher ground to get a better fix on enemy artillery and troop locations. Incoming fire of all types was intense and well directed, but our men pulled back with no injuries. The major concluded that they were facing a division or more.

Hayes reported back to regimental HQ to inform Colonel Cameron of the situation. Not long after Hayes's return, General Eddy, the ultimate decision maker on our movements and timetables, showed up because wanted to hear the major's assessment. The XII Corps commander was skeptical of what he heard, so the major offered to take him to the river bank to see for himself. The general agreed, and they climbed into his jeep and headed to the lookout post. To Hayes's great consternation, the whole area was a picture of tranquility. The river was calm, the birds were chirping, and there was no evidence whatsoever of a hostile force. In fact, General Eddy's response was, "Hell, there are no Germans out there. Let's get underway." He ordered Colonel Cameron to execute a hasty crossing of the Moselle River at Pont-à-Mousson.

On a divisional scale, the plan to be executed over the next few days was to divide our assigned area into sectors, cross the river from accessible fording areas, swing around to the south, and attack the city of Nancy, where the Germans were known to be in force. The 317th Infantry Regiment was to cross in the vicinity of Pont-à-Mousson, which was ten miles north of Nancy, and the 318th was to cross at Millery, about six miles south of us. Our two regiments would then swing around in a large U-turn and approach Nancy from the east. The 319th was to attack from the west, putting the city in a military vise. The plan was predicated on minimal opposition on the way to Nancy.

Crossing the Moselle River, September 5, 1944

We reached Blenod-les-Pont-à-Mousson, a small town on the west bank of the Moselle, during the evening of September 4 with orders to cross the river. Rather than risk a night crossing, General McBride decided to launch a surprise attack the following morning. Our regimental commander, Colonel Cameron, met with the battalion commanders just before midnight, September 4, and outlined the plan for the crossing. The area across the Moselle in which we wanted to establish a bridgehead was dominated by Mousson Hill, across from Pont-à-Mousson, and Hill 358, which is about three thousand yards north of Mousson Hill. The success of the attack was based on the seizure and control of those two hills.

We would normally send out patrols before moving on an objective, but moving speedily and maintaining momentum was deemed important by General Eddy, so his orders trumped our normal protocol. Patrols went out in the dark only to reconnoiter good crossing sites. Colonel Cameron was assured of air and artillery support on the objectives.

Our regiment of twenty-five hundred men formed a line covering roughly two and a half miles, running north and south along the west bank of the river. We were to attack as individual battalions, in coordination with one another, rather than as a divisional unit. My battalion was to move out from Blenod-les-Pont-à-Mousson; 2nd Battalion was to cross at a small town called Vandieres, at the north end of our line; and 3rd Battalion was to reconnoiter for a good crossing point at Pont-à-Mousson, which was between us. After crossing, 3rd Battalion would fall in behind our 1st Battalion to reinforce us.

Able Company was at full strength, with 6 officers and 189 enlisted men. In our sector, the river snaked back and forth, and had wooded plateaus and villages on each side. Running generally parallel to, but in a straight line west of the river, was a concrete-lined canal. The concrete rose up to within about four feet of the top of the dirt banks. Between the canal and the river was flat open space spanning from several hundred to a thousand yards, giving the enemy excellent visibility and fields of fire against anyone trying to traverse the gap.

We got the word to move out at 1000 on September 5. The promised air support never materialized. After three concentrations of artillery high explosives and smoke prep fire— considerably less than the colonel had expected—we moved to the canal. Charlie Company was to cross the canal, which was passable, dash across open terrain, then cross the river to establish a bridgehead. My platoon, along with others, was to provide covering fire. We took positions on a pile of slag next to a burned-out factory, which gave us some high-ground advantage. It was a clear, sunlit day.

Charlie Company made it across the canal, but as it got partway across the open area, the Germans opened up with machine guns. The company ended up being pinned down the rest of the day, unable to move. As long as the Charlie troops stayed down, they took minimal casualties. They were able to withdraw as soon as it got dark, at which time our company also withdrew back behind the canal.

Our two sister battalions fared about the same. All encountered variations of heavy artillery, mortars, and machine gun fire. As the day wore on, after repeated attempts, both battalions actually got

51

men across, but were forced by heavy enemy fire to withdraw back to the west side.

Just before midnight, 1st Battalion received word that we were to try to cross the river again. We moved out along the same route we had taken before, and we made some headway this time. The Germans detected our movement, so by 0300 we were taking heavy machine gun and mortar fire. We withdrew back to the canal. To say that the crossing had not gone as planned is an understatement.

On the morning of September 6, Colonel Cameron received situation reports from all units except the 1st Battalion. The lack of any communication from one of his units was a sure indication that something was amiss, so he dispatched Major Hayes to 1st Battalion command post (CP) to find out what was, or was not, going on. Artillery and mortar fire were continuous around the battalion CP, and when Hayes reached the area, he was alarmed to find that no sentries had been posted and the staff was in disarray. There was an obvious command void. He located Lieutenant Colonel Norman, who had been an instructor at Ft. Benning specializing in river crossings, and determined right away that he was disoriented, traumatized, and in no shape to command troops. Hayes pulled aside Major Burnett, the battalion executive officer, a bald-headed man whose nickname was Curly, and told him that he was going to recommend that Colonel Cameron relieve Norman and turn the battalion over to him.

As Major Hayes headed back to Regiment, his jeep driver had to dodge artillery all the way. Hayes informed his boss of the situation. The colonel told him to have the driver take both of them back down to 1st Battalion so he could meet with Norman in person before making an important decision on a command change. The two men rode back down the dangerous road to the 1st Battalion CP, where Cameron asked a few brief questions of his subordinate and concluded that a change was indeed necessary. Command of the battalion was turned over to Major Burnett and Colonel Norman was brought back to the rear, out of harm's way. I trust that he recovered, but we never saw him again.

We were told to dig in and await further orders. We were not given any information as to the status of other units or what our next move might be. We just knew that no one had made it across successfully this time, but one way or another we were going to have to cross this river. I dug a foxhole into the side of the canal between the concrete and ground level. The enemy made no aggressive moves, but they continually harassed us with artillery, including an occasional shell into or around the canal to keep us alert.

It was now early afternoon on September 6. After spending most of the previous day and night shooting at an enemy that I really couldn't see, as well as trying to stay clear of his return fire, I was hungry. We certainly were not going to have hot chow brought up from the rear any time soon, so I decided it was a good time to break out the K-ration breakfast I had been carrying with me. I opened the small cardboard box, pulled out a can of ham and eggs, opened it, and proceeded to heat it on the small portable burner that I had acquired. Next, I placed the burner on the bank above my head to heat the coffee that I had poured into my canteen cup. I was just getting set to savor this gourmet meal in peaceful solitude when I heard the unmistakable sound of a German shell coming in. By now we could tell from the sound of an artillery shell about where it was going to land, and I knew this one was going to be close. I ducked down into my foxhole and waited. The shell landed on the canal bank across from me and blew shrapnel, concrete, and dirt everywhere. As the dust and smoke settled, I looked down at my ham and eggs. They were covered with black soot. I heard a trickling sound above my head and looked up to see that my hot coffee was draining out of a shrapnel hole in my canteen cup, only a few inches above my head. The Germans had ruined my breakfast and I was *mad.* I scraped the soot off of my ham and eggs and ate them anyway, with only a couple of swallows of coffee instead of the full cup that I had been so looking forward to enjoying at my leisure.

At the platoon and company level, we still did not know the strength and determination of the enemy we were facing. As had happened frequently during our clearing operations, our initial thought was that we had encountered a small group of dedicated rear-guard troops.

When Generals Eddy and McBride realized that they had miscalculated the strength of the German forces, their plan for a quick assault on the city of Nancy had to be postponed. Instead of following their usual pattern of retreating and leaving a rear guard for harassment, this time the Germans had established solid defensive positions and were prepared to put up a fight. The fact was, there were five to six thousand German soldiers dug in east of the river. Many of them were young and almost fanatical. They were augmented by elements of the 3rd and 15th Panzer Grenadier divisions, elite troops who had been brought up from Italy. They were experienced and well armed, with good heavy weapons support, including tanks. In addition, elements of the 92nd Luftwaffe Field Regiment had been brought up from Nancy to help defend the position. Moving our division across the Moselle was going to be an operation all its own.

My platoon ended up staying in the canal banks for a couple more days, then moved back with the rest of the battalion to the safety of a tree line. In typical military fashion, we were given minimal information about what was going on or when we would try again to cross the river.

The Germans knew we were there and sent over a steady stream of artillery shells. Though we had few injuries, we couldn't figure out how they seemed to know just where to place their fire. This mystery was solved when someone figured out that a German soldier was hidden in one of several smoke stacks just behind the tree line where we were located and he was spotting artillery for the other side. He was taken out and we were able to move without being so closely shadowed.

We waited for orders. The need to regroup caused by a much larger-than-expected enemy force was only partly the cause of the delay. The low-fuel rumor proved to be true. What had been a minimal supply a few days before was now depleted. The primary port supplying the armies in northern France was Cherbourg, where the Normandy invasion had been made on June 6. We were now four hundred miles inland. The armor guys a few miles behind us had run completely out of fuel, and our artillerymen were at times rationing shells. General Patton had been haggling with General Omar Bradley over resupply. Bradley had to decide between Patton and General Bernard Montgomery, commander of the British and Canadian forces, as to who would receive the first resupply of the essential commodity. Montgomery won; we would receive our supply a few days later. To try another crossing of the river without heavy armor and artillery support would be foolish. After a few days' wait, the support guys finally received gasoline, artillery, and maintenance parts for their equipment.

During the lull, Major Hayes, at the behest of Colonel Cameron, took on the task of finding a better crossing site for our next attempt. Hayes spoke fluent French, and, in talking to some of the locals, was referred to a French priest who told him that the best place to cross was just below the town of Dieulouard. After Hayes reconned the area, it was decided that this would be the ideal crossing point.

At 1700 on September 11, the division received orders to move out early the next morning and cross the river. The 80th Division was responsible for an eight-mile stretch of the front line, from Pont-à-Mousson south to Millery. Our regimental assembly area and jump-off point was to be in the vicinity of Dieulouard. The 317th Infantry Regiment was to seize the high ground across the river east of Dieulouard. The 318th, minus one battalion, was to cross later and move to the high ground east of Pont-à-Mousson. This would put five battalions of infantry in place to form a bridgehead on the east side of the river. The engineers would provide assault boats and build light bridges to get the infantry across. They would then follow up with the construction of pontoon bridges to allow trucks and heavy armor to cross after the bridgehead had been established. The Moselle had a bend to the southwest at Pompey, where the 319th Infantry Regiment was to cross.

Following the anemic, failed attempt on September 5, support for the crossing was beefed up considerably. We were to be supported by nine battalions of artillery, including a battalion of 8-inch field guns. American fighter-bombers of the XIX Tactical Air Command were to bomb Mousson hill at 1715. All troop movements prior to jump-off were to be made during the hours of darkness.

We left our position at Jezainville at 0100 on September 12 and traveled two miles south to the assembly area. Though it was the middle of the night, everyone was very alert, and nerves were tense. We lined up at the base of a hill and awaited the signal to move out. Just above our heads was a row of forty.30-caliber water-cooled medium machine guns. The heavy artillery was not far behind. A steady light rain was falling.

One lone machine gun opened fire at 0400, which was the signal for the artillery to commence fire and the infantry to move out. Within seconds, the noise was so indescribably deafening that many of my men were frozen in place. I had to go along and literally pull them to their feet and get them moving forward.

The Germans responded with their own artillery, and we soon had a battle on our hands. We crossed the canal and moved into the open area where Charlie Company had been pinned down a few days earlier. We were supposed to be the lead platoon in our sector, but someone had gotten ahead of us and our advance was halted. I got my platoon down and told my men to sit tight while I went forward to see what the problem was.

The company commander, Lieutenant McCrary, had disappeared and we were out of position. I ran across some open ground and found the next senior man in the company, 1st Lieutenant Phil Spalding. As I pounded forward, I heard the snap of bullets going by, but I kept running. I found Spalding and told him I was sure we had gone too far north. With the CO gone, somebody needed to lead us to our assigned crossing station.

"I don't know what happened to McCrary. Are you willing to take responsibility for leading us back to the right position?" I asked.

"No, I'm not."

"Well, I am. I am going to take us back to the south until we either find our crossing point or locate the CO."

I found Lieutenant McCrary as we moved south. He said that an artillery shell had exploded next to him and, though he was not hit, he had been knocked unconscious. Other than a ringing in his ears, he was okay. We got things straightened out; he resumed command and we made it to the river.

When my platoon arrived at our assigned crossing place, there were four pontoon boats on the bank. Sergeant Fabrizio and I had our platoon load up and push off to paddle toward the opposite bank, fifty yards away.

My platoon of landlubbers was still trying to get their rowing strokes synchronized when a mortar round exploded just behind us. Every boat crew was instantly transformed into an Olympics rowing team, and we reached the bank in what had to be record time.

So far, my platoon had taken no casualties. We landed on the bank unopposed, set up a defensive perimeter, and waited for the rest of the company before moving on.

The rest of the battalion made it across by 0650. Our next assignment was to take a hill about a half mile to our front. The village of Bezaumont had been set ablaze by thirty rounds of white phosphorous from our artillery fire, which provided a marker to guide our advance through the darkness.

The battalion moved forward, up the hill and across the plateau, until we were on our objective. We met some resistance, but, other than firing artillery and mortar rounds, the Germans really did not put up much of a fight. Moving across under the cover of darkness, the heavy artillery prep fire, and the light rainfall had worked to our advantage. Also, it later came to light that this particular area was the boundary between two German divisions and thus was not heavily outposted.

Our battalion took the high ground, Hill 382 (also known as Landremont), which was just outside of Bezaumont. By 0830, all three battalions in our regiment had reached their objectives; 2nd Battalion had taken St. Genevieve ridge, and 3rd Battalion was on the high ground across the little valley south of us near Autreville-sur-Moselle.

We dug in with some men digging foxholes and others simply occupying artillery craters or foxholes left by the Germans. I checked with my squad leaders to make sure they were positioning their men properly and setting up outposts, and then I sent a carrying party down the hill to get K-rations and ammo.

After getting my men into position, I set about digging my own foxhole. As I retrieved my trenching tool, I looked down at the suspenders that I wore to hold my ammo belt around my waist. The end of each strap stuck out a few inches and I had three bullet holes in one of the ends—souvenirs of the enemy rounds I had heard snapping past me in the early morning hours. I was very fortunate.

We had been up most of the night of September 11–12. Except for incoming artillery shells and some sporadic small arms, we did not have any major contact during the remainder of the 12th. We had been told to dig in and wait, so we did.

No one could really let his guard down at any time. We were sure that the enemy was watching and calculating, but we did not know where they were, how many there were, or how heavily they were armed. The terrain was such that a unified front was not possible. Each company and platoon had its own area of responsibility, and smooth coordination between units was not really feasible. It was a very tense time.

The terrain we were occupying consisted of two plateaux 1,100 to 1,200 feet in elevation (the hills were named by meters of elevation), mostly smooth ground with clusters of bushes and trees, and wooded areas on the slopes rising up to the ridges. The hill on which my battalion and 2nd Battalion were located was sort of L-shaped, with several villages, including Ste. Genevieve and Loisy to the north and, along the east-west base of the L, Bezaumont and Landremont. Ville au Val was nestled into the base of the ridge below. About two miles to the north of us was a dense forest, Foret de Facq. Only a thousand yards north of 2nd Battalion, this was the command post and assembly area for the German forces we were facing. It was a great place to hide.

To our south was a gently sloping valley that ran east–west along the base of the L; it was a few hundred yards in breadth. Across the valley was another plateau, which somewhat mirrored ours, except that it was more heavily wooded. Two villages, La Côte Pelée and Falaise, were on the front of the opposing ridge Autreville-sur-Moselle, occupied by 3rd Battalion, was to the south near the river.

Just before noon on September 12, General McBride ordered two battalions of the 318th Regiment to cross as the second wave. They came in behind us and set up a perimeter on the reverse slope of our hill. McBride also issued orders for the pontoon companies to erect a heavy bridge as quickly as possible in order to bring the armor to the bridgehead. The bridge exited at the village of Le Pont du Mons. By midnight of September 12–13, two companies of the 702nd Tank Battalion, the 313th Field Artillery Battalion (105mm howitzers), and several antitank guns and towed 3-inch tank destroyers were in the bridgehead. Their timely arrival was pivotal in preventing a disastrous sequel to our first crossing attempt.

The afternoon of September 12 was fairly quiet, but the early morning hours of the 13th more than made up for it. The Germans showed their hand as they mounted a savage attack north of us at about 0100 hours. They came rolling out of the Foret de Facq with tanks and infantry, headed for our just-completed bridge. The brunt of their assault was along the road leading to the bridge, which was guarded by the 318th Regiment, but they also attacked our 2nd Battalion on St. Genevieve ridge.

Confusion and chaos reigned on both sides throughout the early morning hours as the Germans steadily overpowered our forces and pushed our units off of the high ground at Ste. Genevieve, Bezaumont, and Loisy. By daybreak on September 13, the Germans had advanced to within one hundred yards of the bridge.

From our position, we could hear the battle raging along the road at the bottom of the ridge to our west, but Able Company had no contact initially. We began to take small arms fire from the north at 0500 on the 13th. It was still dark and foggy, so we had to return fire toward the muzzle flashes of rifles and machine guns, not knowing whether this was going to be a small arms episode or the beginning of an attempt to overrun our position. Our assignment was to guard the edge of a ridge, so anyone who wanted to come after us would have had to climb a slope right into our guns with little cover, but safety from any quarter was not assured in the least. The battle, for us, did not escalate beyond small arms and random artillery fire.

General McBride ordered a counterattack at 0930. The all-out attack by the enemy to take the bridge had left them depleted, both of men and material. The counterattack, led by the 4th Armored Division, which had just made it across the bridge, and the remaining infantry was a success. What remained of the spent enemy forces were pushed all the way back to the Foret de Facq. By early afternoon the ground to the west and north of us that had been lost was recaptured and the original bridgehead was secure.

The historical accounts say, "Two companies of the 317th had maintained their hold on Hill 382 throughout the night and into the next day. . . ." Ours was one of those companies.

A Commander Is Lost

Just prior to the tug-of-war overlooking the bridgehead, the 80th Division artillery commander, Brigadier General E. W. Searby, moved onto St. Genevieve Hill with the 2nd Battalion, 317th Infantry. He liked to see what was going on at the front and it was not uncommon for him to get into a jeep with his aide de camp, Lieutenant Hinndeman, and move, incognito, among the infantry his guns were supporting to see where his rounds were landing. In this case, he and the lieutenant made it across the river and up to Mt. Mousson with the remaining one hundred men of the 2nd Battalion. They took cover in the ruins of an old castle. It was an ideal observation point, and they ended up calling in rounds on targets all around them, knocking out several enemy tanks in the process. (The artillery forward observer—FO—assigned this duty had not shown up.)

When the Germans pushed 2nd Battalion off of the hill in its run for the bridge, the general and his aide were left to fend for themselves. The second day they were there, a tank crested the hill as it approached the castle ruins. Though it had lost a tread and couldn't move, it opened fire with its machine gun at the stone wall providing cover for the two men. The pair stayed down until the general finally lost patience, grabbed his M1, and said, "I am going to get rid of that son-of-a-bitch." He stood up to return fire and was cut in half by the machine gun. The lieutenant lived to give a first-hand account of the ordeal. Not many generals spend time on the front lines, and most make it back home.

For most of the five infantry battalions and armor, it had been a bloody, calamitous battle as small groups of German soldiers breached and overran platoon and company defenses, both sides capturing prisoners and engaging in heavy small arms fire at close range. Our regiment and the 318th ultimately prevailed, securing and then defending the bridgehead, albeit at a high price. This was the most vicious, head-to-head combat that our division had faced since we set foot on French soil, but Able Company had been out of the line of the main battle and had not fared too badly. We had 179 men and 5 officers, with no KIAs. Nevertheless, in not too many hours hence we would be contributing more than our share of blood to the cause of defending the bridgehead and freeing Europe from Nazi domination. In the meantime, we were ordered to seize more ground.

**

At 1100 on September 14, 1st Battalion was ordered to move east about four miles, away from the scene of the intense battle area near the river to Hill 340, near Serrieres. We were hit by heavy artillery on the way and had several men wounded, but we reached our objective at 1830 and dug in.

We spent the night awaiting further orders, and at 0800 on September 15, we were ordered to return to the vicinity of our original position near Landremont to reinforce 2nd Battalion. We marched the four miles back, escorted by the tanks and tank destroyers. We got there at about 1100 and surprised the Germans, who were at the base of the hill preparing for an attack. They realized that they were caught in a trap and withdrew in a brief but intense gun battle.

Pfc Charles Simcox, from another platoon in Able Company, was later awarded a Distinguished Service Cross for bravery in action during this battle. He killed two Germans he caught as they set up a machine gun, and pursued and killed a third German. Then, with a captured machine gun, he eliminated four more of the enemy. Later in the evening, while on patrol, he fired on a seven-man German patrol, killing several, but he was seriously wounded himself.

No one knew at the time that Simcox would later be awarded the army's second highest award for bravery, but, then, no one was thinking about medals. We just wanted to win the war and go home, and that meant killing or capturing the enemy. I don't know of anyone I served with who enjoyed shooting another human being. The Germans started this mess and set the bar; we were doing what we had to do.

We moved up the slope in pursuit and eventually got into position on Landremont Ridge. Once again, my platoon had responsibility for guarding against an assault overlooking a ridge.

Third Platoon was in a similar situation, although a little further back from the ridge and in a more vulnerable position. We hadn't been in place long before an American tank appeared near

Pfc Ray Patterson, a squad leader in the platoon. His squad was spread out, occupying foxholes and craters, in perimeter defense. The tank pulled up close to the edge of the hill, fired one round, and then the crew all jumped out. They looked around and took stock of their surroundings, then got back in. The tank then began to back up slowly through the mud, down a slight incline towards three World War I craters, each occupied by members of the squad. The men in the craters didn't want to leave their positions and expose themselves to the enemy, so they yelled at the tank to stop, but to no avail. Just short of the first crater, it finally got bogged down in the mud and stopped. The crew bailed out again and disappeared. Within seconds, three artillery rounds landed, one in each of the craters. The Germans apparently had the craters zeroed in. Some of the men made it and some didn't.

Mounted on the turret of the abandoned tank was a .50-caliber machine gun. That night, Pfc Patterson recruited another man to help him pull the machine gun off of the tank. They took it and the ammo belts back to their respective foxholes. The next morning they decided it would be a good idea to replace the tracer rounds with regular bullets so the enemy could not track their location when they opened fire.

They were working on the belts when an unseen machine gun suddenly opened up on them. Ray was exposed, so he dove behind some thick bushes. He hugged the dirt while bullets snapped overhead, kicking up the dirt and tearing up foliage all around him. He heard one round slam into the trunk of a bush above his head. Then the firing stopped. He hesitated, then looked up to see a bullet hole three inches above his helmet.

"Are you okay, Pat?" one of his buddies hollered.

"Yeah, I'm okay, but I won't be okay long if I stay here. I'm going to make a run for it."

He grabbed the ammo, dashed for his foxhole, and dived in. He and his buddy planted the machine gun on the edge of their foxhole, fed in the belt, and opened fire in the direction of the enemy machine gun, tracers be damned. They held the trigger down and kept feeding in ammo until the barrel got so hot that the gun would not fire any more. Ray never knew who he hit, or what he hit, but the enemy machine gun remained silent.

As the fog continued to clear, members of 3rd Platoon could tell that the Germans they were facing were using a tunnel to good advantage. They fired from the top of the hill they were on, and then, as their fire from the hill withered, they fired from the side of the same hill as the troops repositioned themselves. The GIs held their ground while the two sides exchanged fire on and off throughout the day.

In addition to our own sporadic small arms fire, we heard sounds of a tank battle at the north end of the ridge. At about 1300, the Germans had launched another attack on Hill 382, sending fifteen tanks south from Foret de Facq. Our tank destroyers— vehicles that looked like tanks but were lighter, more maneuverable, and had higher-velocity guns than our Sherman medium tanks—drove over the ridge and knocked out nine of their tanks, forcing them to retreat back into the forest.

Holding and Waiting

With the exception of our four-mile march on the September 14 and return on the 15th, the elements of 1st Battalion were in a defensive posture. When we returned and took up positions on the 15th, a contingent of Germans probed and harassed Charlie Company. They kept coming in from a heavily wooded knoll a few acres in size off to our one o'clock position. Charlie Company pushed back without taking many casualties, but it was determined that we now needed to go on the offensive against what was estimated to be at least a company-size unit.

Late in the afternoon of September 16, Baker Company was ordered to move into position and push the Germans off of the knoll. Baker attacked at 1820 hours and had a fierce battle that lasted until dark. The Germans held their ground and Baker suffered major casualties before it withdrew.

Baker Company's bad day did not help the morale level in Able Company. The last few days had been extremely tense. There were still no clear battle lines and, even though most of my platoon was on a ridge, German patrols took advantage of the morning fog to probe our position. For nearly a week we had been engaged, directly or indirectly, in non-stop combat, all day and all night. So many aspects of this entire crossing were random that the troops' nerves were being stretched to the limit. The life-or-death tension of these few days had such a strong effect on me personally that I never again watched a suspense movie. I had enough suspense on that hill to last me a lifetime.

With both of our sister companies having a turn at clearing out this little piece of real estate, it did not take much reasoning power to understand that the next day, September 17, would be our turn.

My platoon guide, Sergeant Lou Chmura, and I had inherited a "plush" German foxhole. It had a rock ledge at each end that served as a sort of bench seat, and it was nice and deep. We knew that the next day was going to be a rough one for our company. I hoped to get some rest, but it was not to be.

It rained all night, but I had another problem to deal with. One of our soldiers became delirious, so I brought him into our foxhole to try to calm him down. Every so often, he started yelling, "Here they come! They're going to get us!" We got him calmed down for awhile, and then, just as we were dozing off, he panicked again. Sergeant Chmura tried to get me to let him knock the soldier out so we could get some sleep, but I didn't think that was a good idea. When morning came, my first order of the day was to turn the panicked soldier over to the medics and get him off of the battlefield. When that problem had been taken care of, I took stock of our plush foxhole. The bottom was eight inches deep in water.

The Battle of Bloody Knob, September 17

Thick fog engulfed Landremont Hill on the morning of September 17, and the rain from the night before let up only slightly. We stayed in place while the Germans sent patrols to probe our positions. One such patrol became a small success for their side.

Sergeant Howard Umbarger was in charge of a four-man machine gun squad stationed on the right flank of the company. It had fields of fire down the slope. Like Pfc Patterson, the four made good use of a crater; they used the hole for protection and set up their gun on the lip. Not far from Umbarger's team was a cluster of bushes. He sent his two ammo bearers back for ammunition while he and the assistant gunner kept watch on the slope to their front and nearby bushes. At one point, the assistant thought he detected movement in the bushes and stood up to get a better look. He was immediately shot. Before Umbarger could react, a potato masher grenade landed at his feet. He grabbed it and hurled it as far as he could, then raised his rifle to fire at the assailants, but he found himself staring down the barrels of three German rifles. Understanding that he probably would be shot, he pulled the trigger and heard a dry *click*. The trio of Germans told him to drop his rifle. The fog was thick enough that they went down the slope undetected by friend or foe, and he was taken to the basement of a castle. He spent the rest of the war as a POW.

**

Later in the morning, as the fog began to dissolve somewhat— the rain kept falling—Lieutenant McCrary met with the Able Company platoon leaders. The battle plan for our company was as follows: McCrary would take 2nd and 3rd platoons straight into the woods. I was to wait five minutes and then take my 1st Platoon up through a clearing on our left to make sure the Germans did not try to envelope us from that side. Jump-off time was 1430.

Though battered and bloodied from the previous day, Baker Company was going to attack on our right flank in another attempt to drive the Germans off of the knoll.

We moved into position at 1420 and then 2nd and 3rd platoons advanced into the woods per the plan. After a few minutes, we heard a vicious fire fight break out. I moved my platoon out on schedule. As we headed left and spread out to begin our swing up the clearing, a couple of men from the other platoons came running out of the woods toward me, yelling hysterically that the rest of the company had been killed or captured.

I was trying to calm them down and get some realistic information when I heard one of my men shout, "Here they come!" A split second later, the whole area erupted in gunfire. I turned and ran back toward my platoon, merging with them as they returned fire toward a skirmish line of German troops that was charging at us in an all-out frontal assault from not more than fifty yards away, all rifles blazing. As the Germans closed in on us, one of them altered course slightly and headed straight for me. We traded a couple of shots on the fly, and we both missed. When he got to within fifteen yards, we both splashed down in the mud and took aim. I pulled the trigger on my carbine, but nothing happened. For reasons I will never know, the German soldier did not fire immediately. I knew there was a small berm behind me, so I rolled behind it as fast as I could, completely coating myself in mud. His hesitation cost him his life; one of my men took him out. I grabbed an M1 and a bandolier of ammunition off of a dead soldier and continued to fire.

The shootout went on and on for almost three hours. Groups of men surged forward, then dropped back, maneuvering, yelling, firing at human targets while trying to avoid becoming targets. There was no time for ammo to be brought up, so during the few lulls in firing, dead bodies were scavenged for additional bandoliers of ammunition. Each side traded round for round, slipping, sliding, falling and crawling in the mud, stumbling over, and even taking cover behind, the bodies of the fallen as the rain diluted the blood seeping from their wounds.

My radioman, Justin Baca, was in the thick of it, as was his buddy, Pfc Howard Simpson. Simpson had been slow to pick up combat skills and Baca had taken it upon himself to watch out for him. As they fired and maneuvered side by side, Baca yelled at his charge to drop from the kneeling position to prone. Baca faced ahead to finish an eight-round clip. As he grabbed another clip to slam into the chamber, he glanced over at his friend just as he toppled over dead from the kneeling position. The scene would leave Baca with a gnawing sense of guilt for the rest of his life.

Pfc Edward Joyce saw Delmar Huen, his buddy and tentmate since the training days in Arizona, take a fatal round in the temple as they fought alongside one another. His jaw dropped in disbelief as he saw his buddy's brains come out of the back of his head. Joyce was stunned, but a splatter of mud from a near miss quickly snapped him out of his spell and he resumed firing. He would have to grieve later.

Joyce was Lieutenant Spoerer's radioman, which meant that wherever the platoon leader went, he was not far away. As the deadly rifle fire continued, he became aware that he was not hearing the lieutenant's carbine firing nor anyone shouting of orders. Joyce looked over and saw that his lieutenant was lying on his side behind a tree, head and shoulders exposed. He quickly covered the few steps that separated them and saw that Spoerer had been fatally shot through the neck.

Sergeant Lou Chmura turned to move laterally and was spun into the mud as a burst from a submachine gun sent his rifle flying and tore up his forearm. Unable to man a weapon and bleeding heavily, but still ambulatory, he removed himself from the battlefield, received first aid, and awaited transport to the clearing station along with a growing number of wounded.

A couple of men saw the company commander, Lieutenant McCrary, go down with a bullet through his torso, but the enemy was thick in the area and no one was able to go to his aid. Sergeant Karvonen was also seen falling backwards as a round tore through his shoulder. He was too far forward for anyone to risk a rescue attempt during the heat of battle.

Another of my buddies, Lieutenant Frances Fitzgerald, from Baker Company was wounded in the thigh. Fortunately, a medic was able to attend to him before he lost too much blood, but he thereafter had to fend for himself in the woods until the fighting subsided.

Lieutenant Spalding took a round in the gut. Though he was seriously wounded, a medic, with the help of a couple of Spalding's men, was able to evacuate Spalding to the safety of the company area as the gun battle continued.

With each side relentlessly wearing the other down, losing men one by one, neither willing to concede, we eventually fought to a standstill.

As the overcast skies began to darken, we were finally, mercifully, given the order to withdraw. Word was shouted from man to man down the battle line, and we began our withdrawal, firing as we went.

I was certain that we had all of our men off the battlefield, yet I could still hear the steady firing of a lone M1 rifle up on the line. I yelled out to my platoon and asked who was still out there. It was Baca. Amidst the chaos of the fire fight, he had not gotten the word to pull back. The men on both sides of him had been killed, and he did not hear the order. He would either be killed or taken prisoner within a short time if someone didn't go get him.

I grabbed my rifle and ran toward the sound of his fire. I managed to get his attention over the noise and mayhem, and told him we were pulling back. A squad of German soldiers spotted us. They jumped to their feet and charged at us over a rise, firing their weapons. When the rifle I had picked up earlier jammed, I snatched a submachine gun off of a dead German soldier. We made a weak effort to return fire while running as fast as our legs could carry us back to the rest of the platoon. Miraculously, we made it back safely. The enemy squad, no doubt as battle weary as we were, had given up the chase. We were both fortunate to have survived, and Baca has been very gracious over the years in expressing his thanks for my rescue.

I know lots of things happened that day that could go into the telling of this story, but they slipped from my memory almost as soon as the battle was over. Maybe it was a God-given reflex to help me retain my sanity. I do remember returning to the company area with the German submachine gun. After things calmed down and we moved back into our defensive perimeter, all the troops wanted a turn firing the weapon.

When the battle started on the afternoon of the September 17, our company had 161 enlisted men and 5 officers. At the end of the day, we had 103 enlisted men and 2 officers—a loss of 58 men and 3 officers.

After my nerves settled a bit, I went looking for my buddies, Lieutenant Spoerer and Lieutenant McCrary. I was deeply saddened to learn that Spoerer was gone. He was truly a friend. I was both saddened and distressed that, not only had McCrary been seen falling, but no one could account for him. I hoped against hope that he was not dead or dying in those hellish woods.

I tried to encourage Lieutenant Fitzpatrick as he was being loaded onto a jeep for transport to the clearing station. His thigh was heavily bandaged, but it definitely was not a life-threatening wound.

"Fitz," I said, "you are a lucky man. You just got a million-dollar wound." He just looked at me with a dazed, faraway look and didn't respond; his face was as white as a sheet. I found out two days later that he had died, and I am sure it was from shock.

**

This was a battle that, I suppose, had to be fought, but a mere glance at the carnage wrought over those three days would dispel from the most hardened individual any notions of glamour connected with war. The battlefield was strewn with so many bodies, both American and German, that you could walk the length and breadth of it and seldom touch the ground. As I looked out over the field of corpses, I could not help but think about the terrible waste of lives brought about by war. The pity of it was that the men fighting and dying for both sides were for the most part ordinary citizens, who, at their core, wanted little more than to live peaceful lives, raise their families, and someday bounce grandchildren on their knees. It was hard to imagine that even the vilest despot, standing where I was standing, and seeing what I was seeing, would be able to derive any degree of satisfaction from sending thousands of men to such an abominable fate. I tried but was unable to fathom how much darkness must lurk in the hearts of men who were willing to sacrifice the lives of thousands in order to subjugate free nations to themselves.

**

The next morning we sent a patrol into the woods on what we called Bloody Knob to determine the German dispositions. The enemy had withdrawn.

When the patrol returned, I heard some commotion. I went to see what was going on, and there were Lieutenant McCrary and Sergeant Karvonen. McCrary had taken a bullet through the chest but, miraculously, it went all the way through without hitting any vital organs. As for Karvonen, a round had torn through the muscles of his shoulder, but he would be patched up and recover. McCrary said that a German medic, with bullets impacting all around him, had tended to whomever was wounded, no matter which side they were on. He swore he would never take a shot at a German medic.

Both men had been taken prisoner. During the night, after the Germans withdrew to a small village less than a mile from Bloody Knob, they left the two of them to fend for themselves and moved on. The men found a piece of white material, tied it to a stick, and were making their way back to our hill when the patrol spotted them and escorted them back.

I will never forget September 17, 1944.

69

**

We were physically exhausted. The Germans had been shelling us steadily since our first attempt to cross the river on September 5. The rain had been falling off and on for several days; it was muddy everywhere. There was no respite. We marched in the mud, fought in mud, took cover and caught catnaps in muddy foxholes. We ate cold K-rats in the rain, when we could get them, all the while not knowing when or where the next artillery shell was going to land or from which direction the Germans were going to attack. They wanted the high ground we were occupying, and they wanted our bridge. They were hitting different places at different times, so one unit could be in intense combat, while another unit a few hundred yards away would be left alone. There was no battle line, only high ground and the road leading to the bridge at Pont du Mons.

After only five weeks in France, the reality of men getting wounded or killed was a constant aspect of our lives. I had experienced my share of close calls but had been spared. It was becoming apparent to me that Someone was looking out for me. My belief that I would return home in one piece was becoming a conviction. Some men had a sense of doom about them. I had a chat one night while we were on the hill with our weapons platoon commander, Lieutenant Walter Eisenberg, a big guy who we called "Chief." I never figured out why he was called "Chief." Maybe it was because he sort of looked like an Indian. He wasn't the most pleasant person to work with, but he did his job. He reported to the company commander, so he was assigned to different platoons at different times.

"Gid," he said, "we are living on borrowed time."

"You may be," I replied, "but I am going to make it through this and go back home."

He was killed in action a few days later.

**

Orders were issued for us to move northeast, then return to Hill 340, where we had spent the night of September 14. We moved out at 1410 and soon took heavy fire from Hill 340, on our right, and a small forest on our left. We took cover, returned fire, and

70

maintained our position until dark. Then, for the second time, we returned to our old position at Landremont.

**

I have been asked if I experienced fear in combat. The answer is "yes." But not in the heat of battle. Most of our engagements were initiated by our side. When orders were issued, my mind was completely preoccupied with preparation and planning—making sure every man knew what he was to do and trying to consider all contingencies. The real emotions and feelings did not sink in until the action was over and I realized what we had been through. We took each day and each night as it came, and did not dwell on what was beyond. There was no sense of glamour or heroism. As has been said countless times by countless veterans, the common mentality among all of us was that we had a job to do, and we did it.

Chapter 7
Wounded in Action
September 20, 1944–January 22, 1945

Having solidified our hold on the east side of the Moselle, it was time for our two regiments to move on. Over the next two days we fanned out to expand our bridgehead. Lieutenant Bill Gladden took over for McCrary as CO of the company. The intense battles seemed to be behind us for the time being, but we soon found out that not all of the Germans had moved on.

We moved southeast to the vicinity of Ville au Val, then probed and moved south. Patrols were dispatched to flush out any remaining enemy troops who appeared to be again moving east. I had a close call leading a patrol on September 19 when several mortar rounds came out of nowhere, impacting right in our group. One round landed between Baca and me. I was okay, but the round sent Baca flying with a piece of shrapnel embedded in his knee. The wound wasn't life-threatening, but it was serious enough to keep him at the battalion aid station for a couple of weeks.

On our second day there, which was September 20, Lieutenant Gladden told me to take what was left of my platoon and to "see what's out there." I assembled my men and we moved out. I led the patrol into thick underbrush about waist high.

We had gone only a short distance before a German soldier appeared in some bushes about thirty yards away from me. We saw each other at the same time, immediately hit the ground, and traded shots.

He had a distinct advantage over me. I had an M1, which fired one round at a time, while he had a submachine gun. Within a few seconds, he put a round through my left leg just below the knee, and a second round grazed the back of my knee. I yelled to my men that I had been hit.

Johnny Fabrizio and a BAR man ran forward to my rescue. The BAR man provided covering fire as they ran. They dragged me back to safety while the rest of the platoon covered our withdrawal.

**

A jeep appeared shortly, and I was taken to a division clearing station to await treatment. I was placed on a canvas stretcher in a tent at the clearing station. When a doctor finally examined me, he determined that I had a flesh wound that would probably heal up in a few days. He had someone bandage my wound and I was shuffled off to a corner of the tent, still on my stretcher, to recuperate. (The actual fact was that the bullet had broken the small bone in my leg just below my knee.) The hours dragged on. As I lay on the cot and assessed my situation, I came up with little to be encouraged about. My leg and foot continued to swell, and the level of pain became almost unbearable. No one of any consequence was paying attention to the fact that I was getting worse instead of better. But that wasn't all.

In the tent next to ours was another tent where soldiers suffering from combat fatigue were housed. A few hundred yards to the other side of the clearing station was a battalion of long-range artillery. Every time the artillery batteries fired, the combat fatigue cases panicked and started screaming. So here I was, with my leg throbbing in pain and nothing being done about it, the artillery battery on one side, and the "psychos" screaming on the other side. After two days, I was about ready to move in with the "psychos" and join their chorus.

Someone finally took my worsening condition seriously and figured out that this was more than just a flesh wound. This meant that I was to be transferred to a field hospital located roughly thirty miles behind the front lines. Though it was a portable hospital housed in tents, surgery could be performed there before a patient was sent farther back to a more permanent facility to fully recuperate.

I was transported back in an ambulance. Following check-in, X-rays were taken. These revealed slivers of metal that needed to be removed. The hospital commander, a lieutenant colonel, told me that he would give me a local anesthetic and remove the metal himself. I was still on the same canvas stretcher, which they

73

hoisted onto a table. I was given a shot, supposedly to deaden the area. A nurse took hold of both of my wrists and leaned on my chest with her elbow. I didn't see this as a good omen. The doctor probed the wound and hit a raw nerve, which caused excruciating pain. When I jerked, he looked up and said, "Is that touchy?" The nurse grabbed an army blanket and stuffed a corner into my mouth with an encouraging remark that this would prevent me from breaking any of my teeth. I fought off the urge to plant my foot in the doctor's teeth and ask, "Is that touchy?" He then continued with the procedure.

After a couple of days, it was evident that my leg was still not improving, so the decision was made that I should be transferred to a more permanent facility. I was once again loaded into an ambulance, along with one other man, and taken to a train station where I was placed on a rail car with several other wounded men on stretchers. We spent two days in the cold, drafty wooden car, traveling all of one hundred and eighty miles to Paris. We made many stops of various durations, and from time to time, someone at a stopover opened the sliding door to check on us and give us a few bites to eat. We never got enough blankets to keep warm, and I don't remember how we took care of bathroom needs.

**

"Well, you are about the sorriest looking human being I have seen in awhile," the admitting nurse said with a laugh as she looked me over. I suppose she had reason to laugh. I was still wearing the fatigues I had been issued before we landed in France in early August. I had dropped from one hundred and eighty pounds to one hundred and forty-seven in seven weeks. I had not had a haircut in two months. Everyone in General Patton's army was supposed to shave daily, but I had not shaved in five days. I was also missing one of my front teeth, and I had not had a bath since our little frolic in the river near Argentan.

The first order of business was to get me cleaned up, so the nurse set up a wooden box in a bathtub and I got as close as I could to taking a hot bath while making a mental note to never again take such a simple luxury for granted. I would soon make the same pledge for clean sheets and hot food.

I was assigned a bed, and shortly thereafter a doctor with the rank of captain came in to inspect my leg. He examined it, left, and returned with a set of crutches. Though my leg was in terrible pain and I could not straighten it, he told me to begin moving around with the crutches and to put as much weight on it as possible.

Not long afterwards another doctor came in, picked up my chart, and noted that I had a compound fracture. He lifted the covers and said, "Lieutenant, where is your cast?" He thought I had taken matters into my own hands and removed my cast. "Sir, I have never had a cast," I replied. He threw the chart down and walked out of the room.

It so happened that this man was the Surgeon General for the entire U.S. Army. He was on an inspection tour of the facilities in Europe. He returned with the hospital commander, who was a bird colonel. In like manner, the colonel picked up the chart, looked at it, and threw it down. Then they both stormed out of the room. A few minutes later, the captain—the original doctor—returned, reviewed the chart and said, "Don't you dare get out of that bed," and he left. Finally a corporal entered the room with a broad grin on his face. "Corporal," I said, "what the hell is going on?"

"Well, sir, you are going to get a cast, and I do mean right away," he said.

Sure enough, I was soon wheeled into surgery and anesthetized. My broken bone was, at long last, properly repaired. When I awakened, I had a cast that went from my ankle to my groin. It was to stay in place for the next two months.

When I was moved into a recovery area, I insisted on keeping my boots with me because they were size 13A, a size that was hard to come by. I kept them under my cot or bed at all times. The next morning, I was sleeping with my head covered (it was cold) when I heard someone say, "Adkisson, what the hell are you doing here?" I poked my head out and saw Hargis Carson, one of my A&M classmates. Naturally, we called him Kit Carson.

"How did you know that it was me with my head under the cover?" I asked.

"I saw your boots. There can only be one person in the army with feet that big."

It was good to see a familiar face. We spent an hour comparing notes on our time so far in France and trying to figure out where other classmates were serving. Hargis would later receive the Silver Star for heroism in combat.

After a few days to recover from surgery, I became part of a group of wounded men loaded onto a C-47 transport plane and flown to England. I was in a position to be able to see out of a window of the airplane. The flight was anything but relaxing. There was no turbulence, but I saw nothing but a wall of grey as the pilot flew the entire trip on instruments. When we got close to our destination, he throttled back the power on the engines, and, within a couple of minutes, we broke out of the clouds about twenty feet above the runway for a perfect landing. I was impressed.

We were put on trucks and transported to a bona fide hospital, where I would remain for more than three months. I will never know why it took so long to for someone to determine that I had a broken bone.

British Hospital, Early October 1944 to January 1, 1945

The hospital in England was fairly modern by the day's standards, and it was staffed by Americans who were very professional. I was in a twenty-five-man ward with other company-grade army officers. The fact that we were in a hospital and not on a transport ship back to the U.S. meant that the army expected us to recover and return to duty. Men assigned to this ward had fairly serious injuries, so we did not have much turnover. We spent time reading, writing letters, swapping stories, and playing poker.

If there was a highlight to my stay in the hospital, I would have to say it was a visit from heavyweight boxing champ Jack Dempsey in mid-October. He came through wearing a suit, shaking hands with everyone, and signing a few autographs. To my mind, he was as ugly in person as he was in pictures, but he was big and had huge hands. He moved through the ward pretty quickly.

I have never been much of a poker player, but I participated in an occasional game, and I even won $250 one night—only to lose it all as the game went on. We all read the Stars and Stripes newspaper faithfully to keep abreast of what was happening at the front and elsewhere. We had a British lady for a cook, and I think all she knew how to make was hash, because we had it at almost every meal. To add a little flair to our otherwise drab meals, we rigged a wire rack to hang just above our wood stove to toast our bread.

Those who were ambulatory helped take care of the ones who were confined to bed. Also, as officers, we had to censor mail. All mail sent back to the States by enlisted men had to be censored to make sure there was no information as to location or troop movements. Officers were on the honor system. All we were allowed to say was that we were in Europe. So, all letters from the enlisted ward were brought in to the officers' ward and passed around to be censored. We had to write our name and serial number on the outside of the envelope of every letter we approved. I took this duty seriously and read every letter given to me, but not everyone did. There must have been someone spot-checking our work, because one of the other officers got into trouble for signing off on a letter that one of the troops had written in Greek. In the field, censorship was handled at the platoon level, with the platoon commander reviewing all of the mail his men turned in. This had to be done during daylight hours, as no lights were allowed on the line after dark.

Ward Mates

Days in the hospital went by slowly, with few resources available to offset the boredom. Not much stands out in my memory of my time there, although there were a couple of noteworthy incidents.

One man in the ward had sustained an elbow injury and, as a result, had no feeling in his ring finger and little finger on that hand. There was a skeptic in the group who decided to take it upon himself to find out if he was bluffing. One day, while the injured man was distracted, the skeptic lit a match and held it up to the injured man's little finger. When he smelled burning flesh and saw what was happening, he jerked his hand away and a lively discussion ensued. There was no more question about the validity of his injury.

We had another man who decided he was going to try a little scheme to see if he could get a ticket home. His presence there was suspect to begin with; he said he had fallen down a flight of stairs in Paris, but the details were sketchy. The nurse came in every morning and stuck a thermometer in each man's mouth to take our temperature, left for a few minutes, and returned to record the results. This man, after the nurse left the room, took the thermometer out of his mouth and rubbed it vigorously up and down his leg to raise the temperature. The nurse got a puzzled look on her face as she studied the thermometer, and asked if he felt sick or had any additional pain. He would usually reply that he felt sort of feverish but had no other symptoms. A doctor entered the ward shortly thereafter, clutching a clipboard to his chest and going through a list of questions. The doctors ran tests and hypothesized about what was causing the elevated temperature, but he could never figure it out. The malingerer was finally sent home.

We had a Protestant chaplain that everyone really liked and respected. He made the rounds daily and was very down to earth. He participated in the poker games and was a regular in the bar, though he did not drink to excess. He told me that he allocated ten percent of his monthly salary for poker, and that he donated whatever winnings he had accumulated at the end of month to a British orphanage. There was standing room only at his Sunday services.

The senior nurse in our ward was an older lady named Mingoria. We called her Mrs. Ming. Her bedside manner was a bit cool, but she was a competent nurse and took good care of us. She told me that if it weren't for the Battle of the Bulge, which commenced while I was in the hospital, they would have kept me for another month to fully recuperate. They had orders to return every available man to his unit as soon as possible.

Return to the Continent, Early January 1945

I was processed out of the hospital in early January 1945 and a group of us boarded a troop transport bound for France. We were to be sent to a replacement depot and, from there, back to our units. Once aboard the ship, we were told that little more than a week before, on Christmas night, a German U-boat had sunk a transport with a loss of twenty-two hundred lives, so we were all issued life jackets and small flashlights. The prospect of drowning on a troop ship in the English Channel, considering all I had been through, was more than a little unsettling. I slept—or at least I tried to sleep—with my life jacket on.

We arrived in the port city of Le Havre, France, at about midnight. Our group was comprised of one hundred and fifty men, and the ranking officer was a lieutenant colonel. The colonel told us to stay out of the city itself because our own bombers had mistakenly dropped a load of bombs there, and the citizens were very unhappy with the Americans.

It was bitter cold, and we were tired and very hungry. We traveled on foot up a hill to an army post located on a plateau. The mess hall was closed, but the colonel had someone locate the mess officer, a lieutenant, so we could get some chow. The lieutenant informed the colonel that it was after hours and the staff was all in bed.

"Lieutenant, I want chow served to these men in short order, or I will see to it that you are busted back to corporal. Is that clear?"

We got chow. It was a slice of bologna between two pieces of white bread—probably the best bologna sandwich I have ever had.

We were loaded on French rail cars and started the long, slow trip to Fontainebleau, France, near Paris. It was very cold, and the train made many stops. Early on, someone found a metal container and some wood at one of our stopovers, which allowed us to start a fire and generate some heat, but it was very smoky. At the next stop, we found some stove pipe, which we routed out of the partially open door. At one point, as we went around a bend, a fellow passenger looked back out through the opening and said there were stovepipes sticking out of almost every car on the train. By the time we reached Fontainebleau, we had burned a hole through the floor of the boxcar.

I stayed at a replacement depot in Fontainebleau for several days, awaiting transportation back to my unit. I got in a little sight-seeing around Paris, including an opulent, sprawling hunting lodge built by King Louis XIV and added onto by his successors. We were told it had two thousand rooms.

We never got away from the cold. The last couple of days I was there, a group of paratroopers moved into our building. We had a coal-burning stove in our quarters, but coal was rationed and there was never enough. When the coal ran out, one of the paratrooper lieutenants walked over to a nice, large, ornate wooden cabinet up against a wall, looked it over and said, "I wonder if this thing will burn." He pulled out his hand ax and, Whack! By the time I left, they had burned the whole thing for firewood.

On about the fourth day at the replacement depot, I received instructions to report to the base post office. I reported to a lieutenant, who showed me how letters were sorted and laid out for delivery. After a time, I asked him why he was showing me all of this. He said, "This is your new assignment. I'm leaving, and you're going to take my place as the depot postal officer." I said, "That is not going to happen. I have a platoon of men on the front lines in Luxembourg, dodging bullets and sleeping in the snow. I wouldn't be able to live with myself if I bailed on them. You need to find another man, because I'm going back to my unit." Things were somewhat informal and, as the title would imply, fluid. So I didn't report to an office and request a change of orders or go through any other formality; I simply didn't return to the base post office. Instead, I showed up at the loading area to get a train going north. It was not long before I was headed back to join my men.

While I Was Gone

I was wounded near Metz in northeastern France on September 20. After taking and holding the bridgehead around the Moselle River in mid-September, the 317th Infantry Regiment remained in the region until mid-December, moving from town to town and village to village, gradually pushing the Germans back, just as we had done from the time we landed on the Continent. Only this time, resistance was much stiffer and the casualty rate much higher, as the Germans attempted to stave off the inevitable invasion of their homeland.

Losing men always resulted in personnel changes, but there was one significant change that occurred when one of our officers relieved his battalion commander.

One of our really good company commanders, James Craig, had been assigned the duty one night of disarming explosives that the Germans had planted on a bridge over a river that the 1st Battalion needed to cross. They had blown up other bridges on the river, but for some reason, they had not detonated the explosives on this particular bridge. Captain Craig assembled a small band of men and led the mission himself. The technique was to simply cut the primer cord going to the explosives, so that a lit fuse would burn out harmlessly. In carrying out the mission, Captain Craig realized that the bridge was unguarded, so he was able to take his party all the way across undetected, thereby establishing a bridgehead. He radioed the battalion commander, a major, and informed him that the bridge was clear and that he could bring the battalion across safely. The major said he wasn't coming. After a brief pause, the captain radioed back. "Major, I'm relieving you of command. I'm bringing the battalion across this bridge." He contacted the other company commanders and directed the movement of the battalion across the bridge. The regimental commander supported Captain Craig; the major was removed from the field and Craig became the battalion commander.

We also lost one of our company commanders due to a tragic mistake. The CO of Able Company when I was wounded on September 20 was Lieutenant Bill Gladden. I found out that Lieutenant Gladden had been killed by one of his own troops after I was hospitalized. The story was that he went out one night to check the lines and a new replacement got spooked and shot him. He was a good man.

Chapter 8
Able Company and the Battle of the Bulge
December 16, 1944–January 25, 1945

In the late fall of 1944, Hitler finalized a desperate plan that he hoped would stagger the Allies and help him regain lost momentum. His plan called for several field armies to launch an offensive strike from the west-central border of Germany, driving due west through Luxembourg and Belgium and thereby splitting the British and American forces. He would then turn northwest and capture the strategic port of Antwerp. His generals disagreed with him, but he overruled them and set the wheels in motion. The Germans, after a prolonged artillery barrage, moved out on December 16 in an offensive later to be known as The Battle of the Bulge.

The Allies were caught off guard. Divisions and regiments were shuffled, assigned alternately to one corps and then to another as General Eisenhower and his top commanders contended with the need to strategically deploy massive numbers of troops to counter the enemy surge. Within a few days of the beginning of the battle, the 80th Infantry Division was ordered to move into the small nation of Luxembourg, along the southern flank of the German Army. The division's primary assignment was to maintain a defensive line to prevent any further enemy incursion to the south. This placed the 317th Regiment in the mountainous Ardennes region.

On December 19, the 1st Battalion, 317th, was trucked one hundred miles north from near St. Avoid, France, to a small town above the city of Luxembourg, about twenty miles southeast of Bastogne, Belgium. The terrain was very rugged, the ground was covered with snow, and temperatures regularly dropped below zero. Able Company gradually moved northward, as often as possible, staying in unheated buildings in or near the towns of Niederfeulen, Heiderscheid, Kehmen, and Buderscheid.

December 23 to 26 were especially hostile. The weather was brutally cold with frequent strong winds. Frostbite and trench foot took a heavy toll.

The battalion moved up to Welscheid in the late afternoon of the 23rd, and attacked the town. Just after noon on Christmas Eve day, the Germans mounted a counterattack, which was repulsed.

On a personal level, Private First Class Baca, the man I had helped off the battlefield during the Battle of Bloody Knob, had a tragic experience on Christmas Eve. After he was wounded on September 19, his knee was not the same, so he was made company jeep driver when he returned to the unit. As such, one of his primary duties was to ferry supplies from Battalion to the company. At about 1900 hours on Christmas Eve, he left the farmhouse just outside of Niederfeulen that was serving as battalion CP in order to make a mail run to the company. The temperature was below zero. There were a couple of feet of snow on the ground and, though it was dark, it was a moonlit night, enabling him to maintain some sense of what was in front of him. As he drove over a small hill, he detected movement to his left. Stopping the jeep to get a better look, he was able to make out a small patrol of men in white snow suits moving past him. He started to say something to one of them as they went by, but the man put a finger to his lips to give him the "be quiet" signal. Watching the last man fade into the woods, Baca felt cold chills up and down his spine as he recognized the silhouette of a German helmet.

He made it to the company, where he tried to tell several of the men what he had seen. No one at the company took him seriously, so he offloaded the mail and returned to the farmhouse.

Baca's buddy Chris was scheduled to make the next run at 2200. Earlier in the evening, Chris had been in a very distressed, melancholy mood, fretting over pictures of his wife and two-year-old daughter that he carried with him. He seemed to have a premonition. Baca volunteered to make the second run and give Chris a break, but he was overruled by his sergeant. He settled down to get some sleep while Chris reluctantly left on the supply run. The next morning, when he awoke, Baca was told that a German artillery round had made a direct hit on Chris's jeep at about the same spot where Baca had encountered the German patrol.

Justin Baca was a serious young man, intense and introspective at times. I don't think he was ever able to absolve himself of a sense of guilt over his friend being taken, leaving a young family behind, while he was spared. The guilt was amplified by the fact that he had seen the enemy patrol and had taken no action. Firing on the patrol would have been suicidal, and may or may not have had any bearing on the fatal artillery round, but emotions are not necessarily subject to logic in combat.

The battalion marched to high ground southwest of Kehman early Christmas morning and was ordered to take the town at 0900. After a thirty-minute salvo of artillery prep fire, 1st Battalion came on line and executed a frontal assault. The Germans responded with artillery, mortars, and an intense, non-stop barrage of small arms fire.

The battalion fought all day, but it made little progress while sustaining heavy casualties. Pfc William Brewer, who joined 1st Platoon, Able Company, in mid-November, saw two of his buddies go down as they moved out. Staff Sergeant Elton Mason, his platoon sergeant, got his eye shot out, but he survived. Brewer's foxhole buddy, Private Julius King, from Texas, was moving alongside of him when he dropped to the ground with a fatal round to the chest. A few steps further on, after traveling no more than a hundred yards, Brewer himself was hit in the right side of his abdomen, spinning him to the ground. He was attended by a medic and sent back to a hospital, where he would remain for two months.

The battalion fought all day with no letup, and finally withdrew to its original positions in the late afternoon without securing the town. It moved south to Feulon on December 27. The casualty count for the four-day period was thirty wounded and twenty-two killed in action. Kehman remained in enemy hands until January 21, 1945, in spite of attempts by other units in the regiment to dislodge them.

**

Following a ten-day stay in the Feulen area, Able Company moved on January 6 to Heiderscheid and then, late in the afternoon of January 9, back to the outskirts of Kehmen. The trip involved traveling two miles east by truck, followed by marching a mile or so to set up on the company's assigned defensive position on the high ground south of Kehmen and await further orders.

The troops disembarked at the designated spot and lined up in column formation. As they marched along a road that had been cut into the side of a mountain, they passed a wrecked car up against the hillside—a common sight. As they trudged along in the snow, they heard the sound of the company jeep coming around a bend in low gear. Men casually glanced back and moved over as the driver navigated his way over the snow-covered road in four-wheel drive.

BOOM!

The jeep hit a mine.

Men instinctively hit the deck. The wounded cried out in pain. The vehicle was blown several feet into the air, tossing the driver and his passenger out of the vehicle like rag dolls and sending shrapnel in a twenty-yard radius. The chassis slammed back down as two wheels went bouncing down the side of the mountain. Men ran to their buddies to administer first aid while the call was sent down the line for medics.

The two men in the jeep were severely injured, as were several others, but all survived, save one. The driver had a twin brother in the company who was in the column moving down the road. The jeep hit the mine just as it was passing the twin brother. He was killed instantly by the explosion.

The commotion generated by the explosion led the GIs to a German soldier hiding in the wrecked car. A tell-tale set of wires running from the wrecked vehicle toward the explosion site made it clear that that this man had detonated the mine. Two men were dispatched to take the prisoner back to the rear. Not long after they were out of sight, two gunshots were heard. The guards returned and explained that the prisoner had tried to escape. No one asked any questions.

Within an hour, the company was setting up their new position, trying to dig foxholes in the snow and unyielding frozen ground. They did the best they could.

**

Able Company stayed on the outskirts of Kehmen for twelve days. As often as possible, the troops tried to stay in buildings to gain some relief from the elements.

Reconnaissance and combat patrols were sent out during these stationary periods. No one liked going on patrol, but it was part of being in the infantry. Every soldier hoped that when his turn came in the rotation, he would have an uneventful circuit. The days of looking for excitement had long since passed.

Ray Patterson, by now a seasoned combat veteran, had his share of patrols in the snow. He had begun the month of January 1945 as a private, and by the middle of January he was a corporal. Early one morning he had just been relieved from standing watch on an outpost when a buddy, Sergeant Warren Troup, from the weapons platoon, entered the room of the house in which they were staying and told Ray they needed one more man for a patrol.

"Patrol? I don't want to go on patrol. I've been freezing my ass off on guard duty, and I just took my boots off so I could warm up a little and get some sleep. Get somebody else."

"Come on, Pat. We need you to go with us. The lieutenant and the other guys are waiting. We need to move out." The man persisted until Patterson finally agreed to go.

The patrol struck out in the snow-covered Wiltz Mountain area. The weapons platoon lieutenant was leading.

The patrol route called for Patterson's group to go to a specific road intersection and make a left turn. From there, they were to proceed for about a mile and rendezvous with another patrol. Coincidentally, a German patrol, coming from the opposite direction at precisely the same time, was to make a left turn at the same intersection, which would result in both patrols moving one hundred and eighty degrees away from each other.

The first leg of their route was uneventful. Patterson was beginning to think that they would luck out and have a quiet few hours, but then he heard gunfire to his front. Moving up quickly to investigate, he and the lieutenant found their men at the intersection checkpoint, facing the members of the German patrol. The two groups had briefly exchanged gunfire, with no casualties on either side. The GIs' guns had frozen. In spite of mal-functioning weapons, Patterson's group persuaded several Germans in the patrol to surrender. Those who didn't surrender simply aborted their patrol, turned around, and departed.

Two men in Patterson's group were stationed at the crossroads to guard those who had surrendered, and to be on standby to hold other POWs who might be sent back. The patrol aimed to not only scout out enemy positions but pick up more prisoners. To that end, they selected two prisoners to walk point and act as interpreters.

The patrol made an incorrect right turn and proceeded down the snow-covered road, looking for Germans. Their first conscript was a small, disgruntled man with a helmet so large that it almost covered his eyes, and an overcoat that was at least two sizes too big. His appearance and manner reminded the troops of the cartoon character Sad Sack. He was alone in a ravine in front of a burned out bus barn. The lieutenant prodded one of the interpreters forward to talk the man into surrendering. The squad watched as the interpreter walked up to the edge of the ravine and engaged the Sad Sack character in conversation. Their chat soon escalated into a heated argument. Suddenly, the interpreter jumped down into the ravine, grabbed the man's rifle, and ordered him to get in line on the road. Sad Sack hung his head, grudgingly climbed out of the ravine, and joined the patrol on the roadway.

As they regrouped to continue, they spotted two German soldiers manning a machine gun on a hill; they were behind a tree about a hundred feet away with the gun trained on the patrol. These two enemy gunners had been watching the proceedings and were ready to retaliate if the Americans took any aggressive action. As he came abreast the machine gun, one of the interpreters asked if the gunners wanted to surrender. Following a brief discussion between the two of them, they got up and voluntarily walked to the crossroads.

The patrol picked up a few more stragglers and sent them back to the crossroads as they went, but Patterson's men began to have doubts about their route as they not only saw no sign of the American patrol, they encountered more groups of German soldiers as they progressed. Not far beyond the machine gunners, they passed a chateau set back in among the trees to their right where a group of enemy soldiers was eating and milling around. A short distance on, they passed another group of Germans eating, this time on the opposite side of the road. Neither group seemed to pay them much attention.

Despite a growing uneasiness among the men, the lieutenant told them to keep going. They soon came to an intersection at the top of a small hill. A short way down the road to the left was a village. After some vacillation, the lieutenant decided that the squad would to go into the village and try to secure it.

Near the outskirts of the village a burned-out truck sat alongside the road. The patrol approached it cautiously and flushed out a German soldier positioned behind the truck. The interpreters walked over to persuade him to surrender. The GIs watched as the level of tension rose and voices became louder. All of a sudden, in one swift move, the man stood up, shouldered his rifle, and shot one of the interpreters in the head.

Everyone jumped back, and brought frozen rifles to the ready. Strange as it may sound, no other shots were fired. Keeping an eye on the assailant, they all skirted the truck and approached the edge of the village.

A BAR man was assigned to cross the road and get into position to provide cover for the others. Patterson admonished him to keep his head down or he would likely be shot. The man darted across the road and took up a position behind a pile of frozen manure. (The Germans stacked manure next to their houses to be used for fertilizer in the spring. A larger pile meant a large amount of land, so, a large stack of manure was a status symbol.) For whatever reason, the sentry slowly and deliberately peered around the side of the mound to get a look down the street. A rifle shot rang out from somewhere in the village. The soldier's helmet flew off as he fell over backwards, fatally wounded from a shot to the head.

The death of a patrol member marked the end of the spate of encounters with non-combative enemy soldiers. The party quickly abandoned the idea of taking the village in favor of retracing its steps.

The Americans had no sooner gotten underway than a call came over the radio from the other patrol, asking where they were. The radio transmission confirmed that they were, indeed, in the wrong place. They marched back single-file to the intersection, picked up their original prisoners, and rendezvoused with the other patrol.

**

Following twelve days on the high ground outside of Kehmen, the company received orders to take the town, which was occupied. Emmett McCrary—*Captain* McCrary since he had been promoted on October 1, while in the hospital—returned to duty in mid-January and was back in command of Able Company.

McCrary did not expect much resistance, so he assigned 3rd Platoon to move into the town and the other two platoons to provide cover. They all moved in a column to within a hundred yards, where 1st and 2nd platoons went on standby, ready to move if needed.

It was about 1600 hours. The 3rd Platoon was to approach the town and advance building-to-building as it had been doing.

When the order came to move out, Corporal Patterson, who was supposed to bring up the rear with Private Van Dorah, couldn't find his partner. Following a brief search, he found Van Dorah asleep in the snow. He roused him with a kick in the pants. "Come on, let's go. The rest of the platoon is already gone. We've got to catch up." The man groggily got to his feet and they set off through the snow.

As the first building came into view, Patterson saw that prisoners were already being taken, but something didn't look right. A closer look confirmed that the men with the upper hand were Germans and the men with their hands up were the rest of his platoon. The Germans had hidden behind the first buildings, waited for the Americans to move past, then sneaked around behind them. Fortunately, they weren't trigger happy. Also, they were facing the village and did not see Ray and his partner approach.

"Drop your weapons and put your hands up," Patterson commanded. The Germans did not have to be told twice. They dropped their weapons into the snow and offered no resistance. Guards were assigned as the rest of the platoon completed its sweep. They found a few more German soldiers, but following a few brief exchanges of small arms fire further into the village, they completed the mission. About thirty prisoners had been taken for

89

only one casualty. Captain McCrary gave Ray a generous compliment for his actions, which came as a surprise because the two had had some minor clashes during their training days and Ray had not exactly been one of McCrary's favorites.

On the Home Front

There was one other development in my life at this point. By my calculations, if everything went as it should, I was now a father. In letters back to my wife, I began referring to our newborn as "shim," because I did not know if we had a boy or girl. It would be another three weeks before I got a letter informing me that I was the father of a son, Gid III, born on January 1, 1945.

It was great to get news from my wife that I was a father, but it had little effect on my morale or approach to my job. If anything, it deepened my resolve to return home in one piece and not to dwell on any other options. I never did get homesick or indulge in self-pity, nor philosophize about the whys or what-ifs of war or my part in it. I wondered at times "How did I get myself into this mess?" but that was about as far as it went. No one in our company was any better or worse off than anyone else. We just took one day at a time and did our job.

Gid Adkisson as a senior at Texas A&M College, 1943

Wedding Picture, Thanksgiving, 1943

Gid and Marie at the home place in West Texas, November 1943, prior to Arizona desert training.

Private Ray Patterson prior to going overseas

**Bill Brewer recuperating at a hospital in Cherbourg, France,
February, 1945**

Ed Sprunger; Truck driver in occupied Germany, summer, 1945

Guy Furguiele, prior to shipping out

Sergeant Herb Barwell in Fussen, Germany, after the war.

Lt. Adkisson in Germany, March 1945.

**Lieutenant Adkisson on the family farm holding the author,
December, 1945. Picture taken on the family farm.
Chicken coop is in the background.**

IV. AWARD OF BRONZE STAR MEDAL: By direction of the President, under the provisions of Army Regulations 600-45, dated 22 September 1943, as amended, the Bronze Star Medal is awarded the following named personnel:

GID B. ADKISSON JR, 0533405, 1st Lt, Infantry, 317th Infantry, United States Army. For heroic achievement in GERMANY on 21 February 1945, in connecti with military operations against an enemy of the United States. Near HALSDORF, GERMANY, Lt ADKISSON's company was temporarily delayed by severe fire from two hostile tanks. With disregard for safety, he exposed himself to reorganize one platoon, evacuate wounded, and then advanced to an advantageous position to dire artillery fire that destroyed the tanks. Lt ADKISSON's leadership and courage r flect great credit upon himself and the armed forces of the United States. Ente military service from TEXAS.

Copy of Bronze Star citation for Lieutenant Adkisson

for actions on February 21, 1945.

Chapter 9
Return to Duty
January 22, 1945–February 21, 1945

I arrived at battalion headquarters just before dark on January 22. I was told to spend the night there and report to my company the next morning. Lieutenant Phil Spalding, who had been wounded in the Bloody Knob battle, had returned and been assigned to battalion staff. He was there and had some time on his hands, so he filled me in on the highlights of what had happened while I was gone and brought me up to date. Then he suggested that we visit some townspeople he had met.

"Gid, I met some friendly people in a house down the street. Let's go pay them a visit."

That was fine with me. The Luxembourgers were friendly and pro-American. They were grateful for our presence, and this family was no exception. We walked down the street, snow crunching beneath our feet, to his friends' home and knocked on the door. Sure enough, the people were happy to see us and enthusiastically invited us in.

The hostess offered us coffee and a small pastry. Hot coffee on a cold January night sounded good, so I gratefully accepted her offer, though it smelled a little suspicious. "Friendly people, a little wood fire, hot coffee. How could I go wrong?" I thought. I took a nice long drink and almost spewed it across the table. I didn't know the Luxembourgers spiked their drinks with potato schnapps. After the first drink, I was sure they had gotten the schnapps mixed up with battery acid. Trying to be a polite guest, I forced myself to nurse my portion along. When I had just about finished, Phil, with considerable gusto, asked, "Isn't this great stuff, Gid?"

I could hardly say no. "Yes, it certainly is," I replied,

The hostess immediately responded with, "Oh here, have some more," and refilled my cup. It was as foul-tasting as anything I had

102

ever put in my mouth. That was one social event I was happy to see come to an end.

**

The next morning I reported to my company and rejoined 1st Platoon.

The hospital had been nice and comfortable, but I knew that I belonged with my men, doing what we had to do, for better or worse. The soldiers I fought alongside until I was wounded had been in my platoon in Arizona. We were a close-knit unit, and I was looking forward to reuniting with them. My sense of expectation was dampened somewhat when I realized that, mixed in with the old ranks were a lot of new faces. Like me, some had been wounded, sent back to the rear to rehabilitate, and returned, but as I made the rounds of my platoon and some of the men in the other Able Company platoons, the harsh reality sank in that there were many that I would never see again.

Both Lou Chmura and Henry Karvonen had healed from wounds sustained during the Battle of Bloody Knob; they had returned to the company. Karvonen had been MIA for two five-day periods in November and had been busted from staff sergeant to Pfc for some reason. Ray Patterson had been sent to the hospital for an intestinal problem and did not return until the day after Christmas. Baca was wounded on the December 19, Elmer Roberts was wounded on the December 22, and Ed Joyce had been shot through one of his butt cheeks while in a prone position on the attack the day after Christmas. They also had returned to the company. I asked around about Johnny Fabrizio and found out that he had sustained a leg injury on September 25 that was serious enough to spell the end of the war for him. Sergeant Rufus Smith had received a battlefield commission on November 20 and had been assigned his own platoon. He was wounded in action six days later but had returned and been transferred to Baker Company before I made it back. After the war ended and final statistics were compiled, the records would show that the 80th Infantry Division suffered the highest number of casualties in its history during the month of September 1944.

Charles Simcox, who had been wounded during his heroic actions on September 15, returned to duty a few weeks later and

103

was shortly thereafter promoted to sergeant and then staff sergeant. Sadly, his medal would be awarded posthumously as he was killed in action on Christmas Eve, during the most intense fighting of the Battle of the Bulge.

**

The rains and mud that I had left in September had been replaced with bitter cold, snow, and wind. I quickly learned that the best way to try to stay warm was to dress in layers. I wore two pairs of wool longhandles, wool trousers and shirt, a sweater that my mother had sent me, waterproof trousers, and a field jacket. But I was still cold.

Most of us had two or more wool blankets that we draped over our shoulders when we traveled. If we got into a fire-fight or had to move quickly, we dropped the blankets and maneuvered. When it was over and we had regrouped, we would send a carrying party back to retrieve them. It was common for two men to sleep together, sharing blankets and body warmth. I don't remember any funny comments or jokes being generated by this arrangement. We were focused on surviving the cold and the war; trying to do both when you were on the front lines was anything but pleasant.

The ground was often frozen during this period, which made digging impossible. If there was snow on the ground at night, we would shovel it away and sleep on the ground. I always tried to sleep on my back with my arms folded across my chest, .45 in hand, clip inserted.

Taking care of our feet was paramount. We had at least two pairs of socks with us at all times; one pair on our feet, which were replaced daily with a fresh pair, and one pair that we kept inside of our shirts. I don't know who washed or maintained them, but we got a clean, fresh pair of socks almost every morning when we got chow. More than once I scraped ice from between my toes when changing socks. Parenthetically, the order of priority for delivery of supplies to the troops was: socks, mail, ammunition, chow.

Also, we had waterproof overshoes to wear over our boots. I remember it being so cold one morning that by the time I got my clean socks and boots back on, my overshoes were frozen to the point that I could not get them over my boots. I had to pour hot coffee over them to get them to flex.

**

The 80th Infantry Division was once again attached to the XII Corps. With the Battle of the Bulge winding down, the U.S. Army in northwestern Europe was focused on crossing through the Siegfried Line into Germany. Forces north of us had, after several attempts, made crossings at various locations and we were closing in on the line in our sector.

Several days after I rejoined the company in Luxembourg, I was made executive officer of Able Company. We were moving almost every day, so I immediately picked up where I had left off.

As we had done in France, we continued to undertake clearing actions in villages and towns, only this time we were moving from the outskirts of one town to another during the day, and conducting sweeps of the houses and buildings at night—with no supporting artillery or armor. We employed a simple tactic: we approached the targeted village stealthily, barged into houses, and shouted at the sleeping Germans inside to surrender. We took quite a few prisoners with minimum casualties for either side.

We zigzagged in a generally northeasterly direction. When I arrived at company headquarters, it had just marched to Budersheid from Kehman, a distance of about five miles. After a few hours, we marched to Wiltz, where we spent the night.

As usual, we sought out houses and buildings to occupy. This particular night, we were not doing a sweep, so our artillery FO and I found a vacant house in the town to spend the night. We found a comfortable-looking double bed on the third story. Fully clothed and with our weapons at hand we laid down. We were just dozing off with hopes of an uninterrupted night of sleep when we heard a tremendous explosion very close by. I yelled at the FO, "Is that coming in or going out?"

"Incoming."

By then we were halfway down the stairs. It had to have been an 8-inch shell and had landed about a block away from our house. There were no more rounds, but, rather than returning to the upstairs bed, we spent the rest of the night sleeping on the floor downstairs.

The next morning, at 1030, we began a mile-and-a-half march to Enscherange. The old timers in the platoon tried to keep an eye on the replacements until they acquired some survival skills, but, even with close supervision, they could still get into trouble.

The trip to Enscherange was to be a column march down a road. A few inches of fresh snow covered the ground and the terrain around us was open, so we were not too worried about direct enemy contact. The Germans were notorious for leaving mines of every kind as they withdrew. The engineers had cleared the road, but not the broad, shallow ditches on either side. I gave very explicit instructions to my men: "Do *not* get off of the road for any reason."

We were moving along routinely when the we heard the sound of a mortar round on its way toward us, only this was not a your everyday mortar; it had the sinister howl that a mortar makes when it has lost its fins and is tumbling end-over-end in the air. It could make the hair stand up on the back of your neck. The veterans had heard this sound before and stayed calm. One of the replacements, however, panicked and instinctively dashed into the ditch. The next thing we heard was an explosion, but it was not the mortar round. Our new man had traveled only a few yards in the ditch before he stepped on a mine. I laid my rifle down, yelled at him not to move, and advanced toward him. I carefully placed my foot directly in each of his footprints until I got to him. Stunned and in a state of shock, he offered no resistance as I picked him up in my arms like a baby and carefully backtracked to the road. He probably weighed 160 pounds, but he felt as light as a feather to me. It is amazing what a shot of adrenaline will do. His foot was blown off so cleanly that it looked like someone had taken a meat cleaver to it. He had been with the platoon for three days; hardly anyone knew his name.

**

We arrived at the outskirts of Enscherange a little before noon and set up defensive positions. Emmett called me over to explain how we were going to approach the town.

"Gid, I want you to take two platoons into the town and make sure it is cleared out. I want you to supervise the two platoon commanders, get the men settled in for the night, and then come back in before dark. We especially need to recon the hill across the river, so comm with Battalion is important. I have to come up with a plan to take that hill."

I assembled my men and made sure they had ammunition. Then we moved out. Inasmuch as communication with Battalion was paramount, we had a sergeant from the comm platoon with us, unrolling a spool of wire as we went.

We met no resistance as we entered the town. I deployed my two platoons and set up a command post in a vacant house. We hadn't been there long before the Germans began to drop mortars in on us.

Right away, I got a report that one of my lieutenants had been wounded. No sooner had we figured out a way to get him back to Battalion than one of the troops from the 2nd Platoon reported to me that his lieutenant had been wounded. I called Battalion to update them, and they told me to send the second man back and spend the night there. They would issue further orders the following morning.

The Germans harassed us with sporadic mortar fire for most of the day. To maintain communications with Battalion, we had to preserve the integrity of the telephone wire, which proved to be a challenge. From the direction of my command post, the first fifty or so yards of wire was strung along a stone wall. From time to time, a mortar round landed close enough to this wall to sever the wire, which meant someone had to make a run for it and splice the wire back together, hopefully between incoming rounds. The communications sergeant and I took turns carrying out this task. I don't believe that anybody in the history of the army has ever run 50-yard dashes out and back and spliced insulated wire as fast as we did, but our timing was good; we both made it without a scratch and maintained the all-important communications link with the battalion command post.

The first floor of many of the houses in Luxembourg was built up to accommodate livestock, while the family occupied the upper floors. Such was the layout of our temporary command post in this village. Late in the afternoon, after we got the two lieutenants out and things were beginning to calm down, I told my ranking sergeant that I was going downstairs, like any good farm boy, to check on the livestock. There was no escaping the cold of the house; we could not build a fire as it would be an open invitation for the German mortar men on the high ground across the river. When I got down to the area where the cows were, there was straw on the floor and two cows lay close together—just what I was hoping for. I snuggled down between the cows and had a nice warm nap. When I went back upstairs and told the sergeant about my comfortable sleeping place, he gave me a very strange look. City boy.

While we were occupying the town and attempting to locate the German firing positions on the hill, Emmett and several other officers were working on finding a place for the whole battalion to cross the river. They ended up traveling about a mile and a half north, to the outskirts of Drauffelt, where the 26th Infantry Division was stationed. They found a place just north of town where the river was frozen almost all the way across, with a gap narrow enough that the men could jump across.

As soon as they returned to the battalion CP to write up the order, they came under a heavy mortar barrage. A mortar round landed in the foxhole occupied by Major Craig and the battalion S-3, Lieutenant Clark. Craig became a casualty and was sent back to the hospital. Captain Richard Connors, the battalion exec, assumed command.

Orders came down that we were to move out that night, so we left our positions and headed back to the battalion area. After getting down some hot chow, we left at dark, and marched north toward Drauffelt. We stopped for a few hours of sleep in the snow, then resumed our mission and crossed the river just after midnight. Turning back to the south, we marched a mile and a half alongside the river to the hill overlooking Enscherange—Loch Hill.

Germans had outposted the road, but to a man, they were sleeping on duty. They awoke to learn that they were now POWs. As we moved through the houses that dotted the hill, we rousted out of bed and took captive the mortar men who had pelted us earlier in the day. One of the POWs said that the hill was such a good defensive position that they "did not think the Americans would try to take it."

**

Our next target was the village of Siebenaler, about a mile northwest of Loch Hill. Again, Emmett asked me to take two platoons into the town in the early morning hours and conduct a clearing action. We left at 0100, and, just as before, caught a few Germans sleeping. I think these troops were actually Poles or Ukrainians who had been pressed into service. They seemed to have a sense of relief about becoming captives of the Americans. We brought them back to the company area.

While it was still early morning, the company cooks brought up chow. They used containers, called marmite cans, which kept our chow hot, even in sub-zero temperatures. Of course, when it hit our mess kits, it immediately turned cold, but we appreciated the effort.

One of the cooks, Tech 5 George Neal, had a carbine. When we finished our chow, we turned the prisoners over to him to take back to headquarters. The kitchen crew had brought our breakfast in jeeps, which they had parked just behind the crest of a hill to our rear, and carried the cans the last fifty yards or so. On the way back over the hill, a German artillery shell landed near the small party, throwing Neal to the ground as a piece of shrapnel ripped through his hand. The group instinctively scrambled the remainder of the distance to safety—except for one prisoner, who stopped and ran over to the sergeant. He knelt down, pulled a roll of gauze out of his first aid kit, and quickly bandaged Neal's wound. Then, grabbing the carbine in one hand, he reached down with the other hand and pulled the dazed sergeant to his feet. The two of them jogged over the crest of the hill, the soldier in his German uniform holding onto Sergeant Neal's arm to help steady him. Neal was taken back to the clearing station and ended up in the hospital. Though he eventually regained full use of his hand, he did not return to the unit. In addition to the Purple Heart, he was credited with bringing the prisoners back and awarded a Bronze Star, as noted in the citation, "disregarding his pain, he maintained control of his prisoners and only after delivering them to the enclosure did he accept first aid for his wounds." Not many cooks were awarded a Purple Heart, much less the Bronze Star.

**

We continued in the attack that same day, January 26. Our next target was Neidhausen, about two miles to the northwest, and, beyond that, Dorscheid.

Charlie Company was to swing around to the north and take a wooded hill that stood between us and our objective. They were temporarily held up by small arms fire until they brought up some machine guns and silenced the enemy.

By dark, the woods were clear and the battalion was a thousand yards southwest of the Neidhausen. As before, we moved in under the cover of darkness, catching the enemy by surprise, though this time they put up a fight. We took more than fifty prisoners and killed or wounded approximately twice that many.

Our battalion commander gave orders for each company to set up a perimeter defense in different sectors around the town. Able Company was facing east.

It was still dark when Emmett asked me to accompany him to the edge of town to figure out where to set up our outposts. As we got to the edge of town, we could make out the profile of someone approaching. He was wearing snow gear. Emmett told me to stand inside of a nearby doorway and cover him while he determined if this was friend or foe. I had a carbine, which I had trained on the stranger, and Emmett had a pistol in a holster.

Emmett had been trying with limited success to get rid of his Georgia drawl ever since we had begun teasing him about it during our training days in the States. He got face-to-face with this mystery person and said, "Who the hell are you?" The reply was in German. Drawing his pistol quickly enough to have left an Old West gunslinger flatfooted, Emmett commanded emphatically in his deepest southern drawl, "Git yo' gotdam hands up." I started laughing so hard that Emmett told me, if the German had gotten the upper hand, I would probably have let him get shot while I laughed. We assigned someone to take our prisoner back to company headquarters and continued our recon.

There was only one road into the eastern part of the town, so we set up a machine gun in a ditch at a road intersection on the outskirts of town, in the event that we had any unwelcome visitors.

The sun had yet to come up over the horizon. The Germans did not seem to be communicating with each other at all as to what towns we were occupying, so they made some very bad assumptions. Within a short time, about forty or fifty enemy soldiers came hiking up the road toward the town. When they got close, one of our machine gunners yelled, "Halt." Instead of obeying the command, a German soldier opened fire. Our machine gunners immediately responded by raking the whole column with a long, deadly burst. A .30-caliber machine gun can deliver devastating fire power, especially at close range. Within a few seconds, this group of unsuspecting young men, wearily approaching what they thought was a safe haven, was turned into a bloody mass of dying and wounded soldiers.

The dead lay scattered over the small area, in twisted and grotesque shapes. The wounded writhed in pain and cried out for help. The pristine blanket of snow, covered with bloody bodies, made for a surreal, macabre scene, forever embedded in my memory. One man's stupidity resulted in one of the most sickening sights I saw in my whole time in the war.

**

I suppose it is human nature to assume that the other guy is smart, crafty, and dedicated to winning, but we got indications from time to time that the everyday German soldier was as tired of fighting as we were, if not more so. One night at about 0200, a small platoon of German soldiers in a village, realized that we had them surrounded, so they surrendered. I ended up having a half-hour chat with a corporal who spoke good English. He said that morale was low, and that the men in his outfit knew they could not win. They were low on supplies and ammunition. Their artillery units were rationing their ammunition. (This was evident to us, because we were harassed by arbitrary, unpredictable shellings, of short duration.) All he really cared about, like most of the men in his unit, was going home to be with his family.

We also wanted the war to be over, wanted to go home. I don't think we ever doubted, however, that we would win. In contrast to the Germans, my experience was that we almost never ran out of food, ammo, or supplies of any kind. If we went hungry or ran low on ammunition or supplies, it was because of a battle situation, not availability.

**

On January 28, we were transported by truck to Medernach, thirty miles to the southwest, where our regiment went into division reserve. The 318th and 319th were in primarily defensive positions with occasional orders to go on the offensive. The next major move would be to cross the Sauer River into Germany.

Company Commander

We stayed in buildings for several days of training. On January 31, Emmett called me into the CP and told me that he was being transferred to battalion headquarters to take over as battalion commander. Captain Connors had terrible frostbite, for which he was going to receive medical attention. That meant I was now the commander of Able Company. We were short of officers, so I had no executive officer, but I did have a good first sergeant, Bill Williams, from Tennessee. Bill was a good soldier, solid as a rock, respected by all of the rest of the enlisted men. He also happened to be first cousins with Rufus Smith, the enlisted man who had been given a battlefield commission in late November.

A few days after my upgrade, I was in the chow line, talking to one of the cooks who had landed with our company in August. "Congratulations on your promotion to company commander, Lieutenant. I've been keeping track and, in case you didn't know, you are the twenty-second CO of Able Company since we landed. All but two have been wounded or killed."

"Thank you, Sergeant. I can't tell you how encouraged I am by that little bit of trivia. If you have any other good news to pass on, be sure to let me know."

**

Third Army had a policy of providing every company commander with a bodyguard. When I became company commander, I selected Marvin Glick for this duty. Marvin was a private from the Bronx, about 5 feet, 7 inches tall, and 165 pounds. He was a sociable kid from New York who got along with everyone.

When I told Marvin that he was going to be my bodyguard, he lamented the fact that he was the senior private in the company. I said, "Well, let's do something about that. As of now, you are the junior private first class in the company," and I issued orders for his promotion.

What we wrote in letters was very restricted, so the folks back home really didn't know what our living conditions were like. Marvin's mother asked him in one letter how he liked the camp he was in. In addition to being outgoing and optimistic, he was loyal and dependable. He also took it upon himself to advise me from time to time about troop morale. I remember him commenting to me one morning as we began a five-mile march, "The morale is high lieutenant; all the troops are bitching."

Marvin was my shadow. I never worried about him getting distracted. He had used his gift of gab to con some tank crewman out of a Thompson submachine gun, which he kept with him at all times. His ambition when he got back home was to open a pool hall. He had it all planned out, but I do not know if he was able to accomplish his dream. I couldn't have had a better bodyguard.

**

We stayed in Medernach until the February 5, conducting training in squad tactics, care of individual weapons, firing of crew-served weapons, and other topics. This down time was good for the troops and gave us a much-needed break to rest and recuperate.

The army was using up junior-grade officers at an unsustainable rate, so a program was implemented to address the shortfall. A seven-week school had been established in Paris at which seasoned noncoms who wanted to become officers and met the qualifications could study and receive a commission. Company commanders were asked to submit names of anyone deemed to be qualified for the school. I had one man whom I felt was potential officer material. He had arrived in France with the battalion as a private first class and was now a staff sergeant. He was a leader who was looked up to by the other troops, watched out for the replacements, displayed good judgment, and maintained his cool under fire. It was Ray Patterson, the Rhode Islander who had succeeded in capturing several prisoners around Christmas time. I had him report to me.

"Sergeant Patterson," I said, "I have a proposition for you. How would you like to become an officer? There is a school in Paris, and I can get you in. You would come out in seven weeks as a second lieutenant."

"Well, lieutenant," he replied coolly, "I appreciate the offer, but right now I have flashing lights on my ass so the Germans can have a good target to shoot at. You're asking me if I want to add flashing lights to my head and shoulders as well, so they will have an even better target. No, sir; I'll take my chances where I'm at."

He made it back home in one piece and became a sub-station supervisor for a state utility, so I guess he made the right decision.

**

The Luxembourg people were friendly to us. One gentleman in particular, a gregarious, middle-aged farmer who could manage a little English, took a special liking to Sergeant Chmura, my former platoon guide, who had wanted to knock out my combat-fatigued trooper before the crossing of the Moselle River. The farmer was either divorced or separated from his wife, who lived in town. After we had been in Medernach for a few days, he made an offer to the affable sergeant that would be hard for any red-blooded combat-weary soldier to refuse. He offered to make arrangements for him to have sex with his estranged wife. He promised to personally escort him to her place the next morning. This elevated the sergeant's spirits considerably and was no doubt the source of some lively discussions among the troops. The needs of the army, however, trumped his recreational opportunity, as the next morning he, along with the rest of the battalion, was trudging down the road to Diekirch instead of rolling in the hay with the farmer's wife.

After a few days' stay in Diekirch, we marched to Beaufort, where we stayed in buildings and conducted more training. Beaufort was about a mile from the Sauer River and the southwestern corner of Germany.

It rained steadily for the first few days of February, after which the temperature began to rise, causing an early spring thaw, though cold nights stayed with us. This created a challenge for the engineers as to how best to get us across the swollen, fast-moving river.

Various means were used to get the division across. By the time our regiment arrived on February 14, a bridge had been erected, so we marched to Bollendorf, Germany, to take up positions northwest of the town. We stayed there for several days.

On the morning of February 16, I was told to report to regimental headquarters. When I arrived, the battalion commander, my old CO, Emmett McCrary, informed me that I was now a first lieutenant and had another officer present me with silver bars. McCrary was still a captain. (The task organization rank for a battalion commander is lieutenant colonel.) I got in my jeep and drove back to my unit and was congratulated by my new temporary first sergeant, Sergeant Justice, which was the full extent of any pomp and circumstances. (Bill Williams had been sent back to Ft. McPherson, Georgia, for ninety days of temporary duty.)

On February 17, we received orders to resume the attack to the northeast the next day.

**

On the evening of February 19, we moved into the village of Stockigt, spent the night there, and the next night marched into Halsdorf. Shortly after midnight, we moved to a hill on the outskirts of town.

Each infantry company was allocated two jeeps, one of which was for the company commander. Justin Baca was now my jeep driver.

I decided to make the short trip in the jeep. I told Justin to drive through the woods up to our new position.

Life-and-death tensions tend to heighten people's senses, and I had developed exceptionally good night vision, a trait that Justin did not share. We had to travel with our lights blacked out, and there was no moonlight to help us. We were moving slowly through a wooded area when I said, "Watch out for that tree, Baca."

"What tree?"

Bam!

"That tree," I replied.

The bumper was slightly dented and we had banged our heads on the windshield, but, other than that, we were okay.

Chapter 10
Hill 420
February 21, 1945–March 13, 1945

The Germans left us undisturbed the rest of the night, so we got a few hours' sleep. After early morning chow, Emmett called me over to the battalion CP.

Several hundred yards to our front was Hill 420. Emmett informed me that someone in division HQ decided upon our arrival that we needed to take that hill. The purpose of our meeting was for him to inform me that Able Company had been selected for this dubious assignment.

He pulled out a map of the area and briefed me on the mission, but tactically, there wasn't much to discuss. We were to come on line and move down a smooth, gentle slope and then back up the front slope of Hill 420, which was about six hundred yards to our front and covered with foliage. There were no places for cover and concealment in our path, and no tree lines on either side of the open area to allow us to lay down a base of fire and perform an envelopment. It was an infantryman's nightmare: we would be exposed the entire distance to the objective. We knew the Germans occupied the hilltop, but no one knew their strength level. Emmett's explanation of the mission and battle plan burned up all of a minute. The whole endeavor made no sense.

I looked at the map and then glared at Emmett. I couldn't believe that one of the most competent officers and tacticians that I had served with was actually sending me, or anybody, on this mission.

"Emmett, why are we doing this?" I asked. "You know as well as I do that a squad of men on that hill, and maybe a machine gun, which they will surely produce, will be able to mow us down like ducks in a row. This hill has no strategic importance whatsoever; we are going to lose men, and for what? This goes against all we were taught and all we've learned since we've been here."

"Gid, I won't disagree with you. Believe me, Colonel Fisher [the regimental commander] and I both argued against this operation, but we got overruled. General McBride is insistent on our taking this hill and would not discuss any options. We don't have a choice. But if anybody can do it, you can. I am going to assign you an FO and make sure you have good arty on the hill. It has to be done. Good luck."

I looked at the map, walked over to a tree that provided cover, and studied the hill and the smooth, open ground we were going to have to traverse. My mind began to check off all of the bad things that were likely to happen in the next couple of hours: How many men will I lose? What idiot hatched this plan? Why didn't he bring his staff up here and risk the lives of his own men? What if the Germans have the area registered with artillery? We will have absolutely no place to go except back to the tree line, which could well end up being a mad dash back to safety with the devil taking the hindmost.

As the questions began to snowball in my brain, I mentally grabbed myself by the stacking swivel and snuffed out those thoughts along with any accompanying emotions. I was an officer in the U.S. Army and had orders to carry out. End of story.

I walked back to the table, laid the map down, turned and assembled my platoon leaders for a briefing. I did my best to issue instructions without allowing my voice or body language to betray my sense of foreboding.

We staged in the tree line on top of the hill to which we had relocated in the middle of the night; it was to be our jump-off point for the attack. We stocked up on ammunition, did our equipment check, and got ready.

After some artillery prep fire, I had my platoons come on line and move out. It was early morning, February 21, and the weather was clear—good for the Germans and bad for us.

With one hundred and fifty men, we covered about a quarter-mile front. We began to take small arms fire from the tree line almost immediately, but we returned fire and kept moving.

We had traversed about two hundred yards when two tanks popped out of the woods at our ten o'clock position and opened fire on us. A single tank, much less two, has the undisputed advantage over foot soldiers in any quantity. Unless you have a bazooka or rifle grenade and a shot from the back, without a place to hide, you are a dead man.

Knocking out those tanks with artillery instantly became my number-one priority. Our forward observer was a second lieutenant, a graduate of West Point: he was not the FO that we usually worked with. He and I each had a wireless radio. At about the time the tanks appeared, his radio took a round, putting it out of commission. He told me that he was going back to get a replacement and would return.

Good radios must have been hard to come by because I never saw him again.

The FO's departure meant that I now had responsibility for not only maneuvering my company but directing artillery fire as well. The FO had been talking directly to the artillery guys; I was working with a liaison officer at the battalion CP who then relayed my requests.

When the tanks appeared and my FO disappeared, I called for artillery to knock them out, which would hopefully even the odds somewhat. Within a minute, rounds were impacting all around them. I did my best to adjust fire while I tried to keep my company moving.

In spite of the tanks, my men advanced bravely. I was beginning to think that we might have a chance if the artillery guys did their job.

My little surge of optimism plummeted, however, when I heard the distinctive clatter of a German machine gun to our right front. They had brought up a gun and were firing from the edge of the tree line at our two o'clock position. We were now caught in a crossfire. They had unobstructed fields of fire on my entire company. My choices now were to either eliminate the heavy weapons or get my men back to safety before the whole unit was destroyed.

The air was filled with the sound of the tanks firing; artillery and mortar rounds detonating; and machine gun and small arms rounds snapping, ricocheting, and thumping into the ground, or, worst of all, hitting their intended targets. Dust was flying, soldiers were shouting and trying to move up without being picked off, and the machine gunners were looking for movement.

Though your instincts tell you to find a depression in the ground or a mound to hide behind, there was precious little cover to be had. Each man's only option was to move forward and hope to be lucky.

I was shouting orders, as were my platoon commanders and squad leaders. Men were calling for medics. We had three, one for each platoon, and they could not keep up with the calls for medical aid. I could see men up and down the line dropping and not getting back up.

Staff Sergeant Rasberry took a round in the chest. When Sergeant Patterson went to his aid, Rasberry told him he could not breathe, and thought he had a punctured lung. Patterson yelled at two other men to help him. They somehow acquired a litter, and the three of them carried Rasberry back to the tree line. Even with bullets and mortar rounds landing around them the whole way back, none of Rasberry's friends was hit.

Sergeant Guy Furgiuele, from Pennsylvania, had joined the company in mid-January and been assigned to be Herschel Vaughn's foxhole buddy. As we moved up the hill, Vaughn took a round in his leg, seriously disabling him. He yelled to Furgiuele, who grabbed his close friend's shirt collar, dragged him back from the main line of fire, and called for a medic. The platoon medic, Bill Franke, who was going from man to man to administer first aid, heard Furgiuele's call and came to Vaughn's aid. They got him back to the safety of the tree line.

I called for more artillery to be brought in to our far right, to take out the machine gun nest. To my utter disbelief, I was told that they were out of our artillery battalion's sector of responsibility. So much for supporting arms. I did not have the wherewithal to argue it out with them.

That was the final straw. It was time to cut our losses and pull back. I shouted orders to withdraw.

As I was moving down the line to pass the word to my platoon leaders, a bullet knocked my legs out from under me. I hit the ground and yelled to my radio operator that I was hit. I bent my knee a couple of times, and everything seemed to be in working order, so I continued on. I had my hands full and don't remember ever looking down to check my leg.

I radioed back to have smoke laid down in front of the German tree line. Battalion relayed to me that the artillery guys had no smoke rounds, but they would try to borrow some. After the machine gun sector news, I didn't think things could get any worse, as I envisioned a private jumping into a jeep and driving to the next artillery battalion to pick up some smoke rounds. What they really meant was that they would give the target coordinates to another artillery unit which would send them our way. Thankfully, within a couple of minutes, they placed rounds perfectly, right in front of the enemy, to our right front. There was a gentle breeze blowing right to left, which was just what we needed.

Enemy fire dropped off. The able-bodied troops began to move back, bringing with them as many of the wounded as they could. I stayed in the open and got the company back to safety in the tree line, where we had begun.

After I confirmed that we were thoroughly evacuated, I turned to head for the tree line myself when someone yelled that there was a wounded man still out in the field.

I looked down the slope and could see him about a hundred yards away. The smoke screen was still blocking the Germans' view, so I figured that I had time to get him to safety.

I took off running down the hill and was able to reach him without attracting enemy fire. He was severely wounded and unable to walk. If he was going to get out, he would have to be carried.

I was able to somehow get him draped over my shoulders, get to my feet, and lumber up the slope toward our position. I was completely exhausted. I do not know where the strength came from to carry the man. The smoke was clearing and I was the only person moving on the battlefield, a tempting target for any German who wanted to test his marksmanship. I heard the machine gunner open fire, walking rounds up the slope toward me as I ran. As the rounds got closer, I fell face-down into the dirt, which sent my passenger tumbling off my shoulders and my helmet bouncing forward into a small crater. The Germans must have thought that I was hit, because the firing stopped.

I lay still for a moment, gasping for breath, trying to gather my strength. The wounded soldier was moaning in pain, but I simply did not have it in me to hoist him back onto my shoulders and start running again. I told him to sit tight and we would send out a patrol after dark to get him.

I slowly crawled forward, snagged my helmet, and, when I thought I could make it the rest of the way, jumped to my feet and dashed for the safety of the tree line.

Marvin Glick, my bodyguard, came running out of the tree line to meet me. We heard in the distance, from behind our lines, the launching of several hundred rockets from five of our tanks. This was a new weapon. Each tank could launch ninety, 3-inch rockets in rapid succession.

Marvin yelled, "The Germans are going to get it now!" Within a few seconds, we both realized that these wonderful new rockets were going to be woefully short and were in fact starting to impact on top of us. We were close to a foxhole and both of us made a dive for it. He hit first, and I landed right on top of him.

"Goddammit, Lieutenant, I beat you this time," he yelled as he laughed and attempted to suck some air back into his lungs. One rocket landed so close that we were covered with dirt, but neither of us was hit.

We made a successful withdrawal, including bringing back most of our wounded. It was a costly battle, but we were able to back out early enough to prevent the mission from being a total disaster. Though it seemed much longer, the duration of the whole battle was probably an hour. I had the platoon leaders account for their men while I reported to the battalion aid station to have my wound checked, after which I was to report to the battalion commander.

My fatigue trousers were ripped open and the lower half of the cloth was caked in a mixture of dirt and blood. The medics examined me and said I had a small chunk taken out of the calf of my leg, about three inches in length. There was no need for me to report to the clearing station; I would be sore and walk with a limp for a few days. They put sulfa powder on the wound, bandaged it up, and said they would put me in for a Purple Heart medal.

The casualty list from that day was long. I decided early in my command experience to keep my emotions in check, because I did not want anything to cloud my judgment, but this time it was difficult to maintain a matter-of-fact perspective. I had a lot of mixed feelings. On the one hand, I was proud of my troops. The men of Able Company had performed as professional soldiers. No one panicked, no one froze in position or ran for safety. They stayed cool under fire and functioned as a team. At the same time, I could not help but feel a weight of grief and anger. We had taken so many casualties on a mission in which the chances for success were slim to none and fruitless loss of life and limb was all but guaranteed. Rasberry and Vaughn would eventually recover, but many others were not so lucky. Twenty-nine of my men were wounded, sixteen were dead, and six were unaccounted for. I told the medics not to turn me in for a Purple Heart.

Before I reported to the battalion CO, I tracked down the lieutenant responsible for the errant rocket fire. I was furious. His miscalculation could have maimed or killed a lot of men who had survived a brutal battle. I really laid into him. I think he was a newbie; he did not have much of a response.

I went on to meet with Emmett and the other company commanders. They had all observed the action; there was not much to explain that they did not already know. We sat around a table, and I remember a few minutes of discussion before I laid my head on the table and went to sleep. They left me alone while I slept for several hours.

As I had promised the wounded man, whose name I do not know, we sent a patrol out after dark to bring him back, but we did not find him. I never learned his fate.

There is a bit more to the story of Hill 420. While we rested and regrouped, I found out more about why it was so important to take this hill. Many facts pointed to this being a suicide mission, ordered by a general at the division level. At that time, our battalion was the easternmost unit in Third Army, and my personal conclusion was that some general wanted to take this hill as a feather in his cap. Our regimental commander and battalion commander had protested, but he overruled them, and the mission was on. As we say on the farm, that definitely "stuck in my craw." I did not appreciate it then and, I don't appreciate it now. But there was nothing I could do about it. There were more hills to take and more towns to clear.

Also, someone, probably Glick, wrote me up for a Silver Star. The battalion adjutant downgraded it to a Bronze Star, which I received after we got back to the States. It was not uncommon for award recommendations to be downgraded, but this incident was influenced by a little history of bad blood.

When we were in training in Arizona, we would be divided into "good guys and bad guys" for our war games. The good guys tried to take an objective and the bad guys defended it. During one of our exercises, my platoon was defending a fake supply depot. We were pulled off and repositioned, but before we left, I set up a small TNT booby trap. This adjutant-to-be was on the offensive and his unit reached the objective first. As they were checking out the supplies, he set off my little surprise, providing his platoon with a good laugh. Of course, there was not enough dynamite to hurt anybody, but it got his attention in a big way. He had absolutely no sense of humor, was not well liked, and could carry a grudge as well as anybody. He knew I was responsible and told me that he would get me back some day. He finally had his day.

**

The next day, our unit moved down to Nusbaum. The Germans occupying Hill 420 were ultimately surrounded, with the result being that they all surrendered.

Justin Baca

In addition to a bodyguard, each company commander was given access to a jeep, which was kept with the motor pool. A personal driver was also assigned.

Pfc Justin Baca was my driver, and my radio operator. Though we did not use the jeep very often, I occasionally sent him on an errand to deliver messages or pick up supplies. He seemed to have a knack for bizarre encounters with the Germans while on his jeep excursions.

One February morning, I dispatched him to the battalion CP to deliver a report. He was driving along on his merry way when German artillery began to fall around him. He slammed on the brakes, grabbed his rifle, sprinted to the nearest artillery crater, and jumped in. He ducked down below the edge of the crater as the damp dirt settled from the first round and was startled to find that

123

someone else had also taken refuge there. It was a German soldier, who was also armed and was just as startled as Justin.

Each instinctively pointed his rifle at the other and waited. Either man could have ended the other's life in an instant, but neither could have anticipated what would happen next.

Baca broke the tense silence. "You people are losing the war. Why don't you lay down your rifle and become my prisoner?"

"I know we are losing," the young man replied, "but I am a loyal German soldier, and I will fight to the death."

"What good is it to die for a losing cause?"

"My orders are to fight until the end, and that is what I intend to do."

These two young men, neither of whom had yet seen his twentieth birthday, negotiated over this life-altering decision, while ducking and wincing as the incoming rounds exploded around them.

The barrage ended. They glared at each other in silence. They were at an impasse. Each quietly resigned himself to the fact that the other was not going to relent. At the same time, neither man was inclined to elevate the level of antagonism; part of their unspoken agreement was that they would, in the middle of a brutal war, part in peace. It was a poignant moment, the stuff of movies. Finally, Justin swung around, stood up, scampered out of the crater to his jeep, and drove away. Fearing reprimand, he never told anyone in his unit of this experience until years later, at one of our reunions.

Friendly Fire

We continued to move northeast, making light contact with the enemy. On February 26, I assigned 1st Platoon to guard a bridge at Koosbusch while the rest of us hiked another mile and a half to the outskirts of Biersdorf. Our assignment was to clear the town and move through. The Germans beat us to the punch, however, and we had to take cover from a hail of incoming artillery fire before we could even recon the place. We had moved into a dense tree line on raised ground east of the town and the Germans obviously saw us coming. We did not have attack orders yet, and I was not going to move out until we silenced the guns that were trained on us.

In addition to mortar and artillery fire, they had a couple of snipers who were deadly accurate. The mental and physical reaction to an artillery barrage compared to an occasional rifle shot is greater by an order of magnitude, but if a sniper bullet has your name on it, the results are the same. We had a new platoon leader, Lieutenant McDermott, who had reported in early that morning, fresh from OCS. I gave him a few pointers and assigned him to a platoon. It was a rough way for a green lieutenant to begin his tour of duty, but there were no guarantees that a man could be eased into his billet little by little. Thus, an artillery barrage at Biersdorf was his introduction to the war in Europe. His beginner's luck held up under incoming fire, but then it ran out.

The enemy let up for awhile, but shortly afterwards, a runner reported to me with bad news. Lieutenant McDermott had been killed. Apparently, he had been lulled into a sense of safety when the artillery stopped. He began to move around, offering himself as a target to the sniper. He was taken out with a single shot as he moved across an open area. I barely learned his name.

When I got the word about Lieutenant McDermott, I had already called up Pfc Elmer Roberts. Possessed of great eyesight and marksmanship ability, he was our sniper specialist. This time, however, our antagonists were concealed well enough that even Roberts could not find them.

I got together with our artillery observer and we called for fire on the town.

"We can't do that," came the reply from the artillery battalion. "That town is occupied by the 4th Cavalry."

I grabbed the handset. "Well, you tell them that we are on their side, and have them stop shooting at us."

Nothing changed until about 1600 hours, when Battalion called and admitted their mistake: the Germans had the town after all, and we were going to get the artillery we requested earlier. We waited and watched for the arty guys to give the enemy some of their own medicine. Sure enough, the shells started falling. On us.

"Cease fire, cease fire, cease fire," I shouted over the radio, after grabbing the handset away from the FO. "You are shelling our position."

"That can't be possible. We are firing on the town," replied the artillery officer.

"Why don't you come up here and see for yourself?" I demanded.

"Let me talk to the FO," came the voice on the other end.

After some brief and highly animated discussion, the FO finally convinced them to not send a planned second salvo. We had several men killed and wounded that day. Among the latter was Pfc William Brewer, who had returned to duty from his Christmas day wound six days earlier. He was shot in the leg, sent to England, and discharged from the army. I don't know how many casualties to ascribe to either side. I will say that the "friendly fire" was the most devastating artillery barrage I experienced during my time in combat. I had no sympathy for our opponents, but it helped me to comprehend that when we called back for our gunners to "fire for effect," whatever group of German soldiers were on the receiving end paid dearly.

We stayed on the high ground outside of the town. Enemy fire died down and we moved in, took a few POWs, and bivouacked a half mile north of the town on the night of February 27. As was their pattern now, the Germans were leaving small detachments for delaying actions while they pulled back to the north.

**

The next day, February 28, we were told to get ready to move west to Liessen. Along the way, we took sporadic artillery fire from the west, and I wanted to try to find out where it was coming from. There was a vacant three-story farmhouse about a quarter mile from our position that was a perfect place from which to make a visual recon. I snagged our FO and we made our way to the site, climbed the stairs to the third floor, and pulled out our binoculars. You had to stay as far back as possible from the windows when scanning because there was always the possibility that someone somewhere was watching through another set of binoculars for movement or a glint of sunlight reflecting off of anything shiny. We were following the rules as we surveyed the horizon, when, all of a sudden, we were jolted by the impact of an artillery shell about fifty feet away. It peppered the house with shrapnel and dirt clods. A few seconds later, another shell landed on the opposite side of the house, about the same distance away. The next round would be a direct hit.

Racing headlong down the stairs, our boots hitting about every fifth step, we just made it to the basement when the house was rocked by a tremendous explosion.

It was time to go. As soon as the wood and glass stopped falling, we crawled out of the basement and sprinted away, looking back only long enough to see that the top floor was gone. The round had come through our third-story window.

Good shooting.

**

Artillery and mortar fire were nerve-wracking at the least, and deadly at the worst. They killed and maimed; tore up houses, roads, bridges, equipment; and stopped or impeded troop movement. Tree bursts were the worst. When you were in a foxhole, even if a round landed close to you, you could duck down below grade and avoid shrapnel. When a round detonated in a tree, shrapnel went in every direction; there was no such thing as a safe place. There were shattered trees all over the countryside. In addition to injury and damage, it is not possible to accurately convey the tension one feels with artillery exploding all around. You just stay as low as you can and hope it is not your unlucky day.

I am sure that the largest percentage of our injuries was the result of artillery. One never knew when the enemy had a location zeroed in, with a spotter hiding out, waiting for troops to come into the zone. Spotters also watched for signs of troop presence. Sometimes they employed baiting tactics—firing arbitrarily and watching for return fire from American troops to flush out their position.

If the enemy was using guns with a range of several miles, you could not hear the sound of firing. Once you heard a shell coming, you had about two seconds to respond. As I have mentioned elsewhere, it did not take long to learn about where a shell was going to land, but that, of course, did not give much measure of safety. I remember seeing one man standing next to a halftrack when a shell made a direct hit on the vehicle. I saw his torso and one of his arms fly into the air, but there could not have been enough left of him to put into a body bag.

Occasionally there was a dud. When we dug in, we usually dug slit trenches versus foxholes. One man in our company had a dud land right next to him in his trench. He leaped out and ran to another place for cover and would not go back to his trench even to retrieve his rifle. It was his lucky day.

Mortar rounds had fins and made no sound, so if you were on the receiving end of a mortar attack, there was no two-second warning. There was a "whoosh-boom," and that was it. They just came out of nowhere. The biggest mortars in the U.S. arsenal were 81mm. The Germans had 120mm, which is almost five inches in diameter, and they had a range of about two miles. A mortar barrage could be just as deadly as artillery.

**

On February 28, Captain James Woodside became our company commander and I was bumped back to company executive Officer. He had an air of confidence about him and, though we did not work together very long, my impression was that he was absolutely fearless.

During the night of February 28–March 1, we moved in a black out from near Biersdorf on up to Oberweiler, and back down to Niederweiler. On the way, one of the trucks in our convoy drove off a bridge that spanned a dry creek, spilling equipment and injuring a couple of men. After a brief stop to make sure the injured men got medical attention, we resumed travel and arrived at our destination sometime after midnight.

After we got settled in, I told Captain Woodside that I wanted to take a jeep back to the wreck site and salvage some much-needed equipment. He approved.

I got a driver and a jeep, and we headed back. We loaded all that we could and finally got back to the company near daybreak. I couldn't remember when I had last slept and wanted to at least take a nap before we moved out again. The kitchen crew had set up in a house, and there was a tarp from one of their 6x6 trucks folded up in the corner of one of the rooms. I told the cook that I was to going lie down on that tarp and rest for a few minutes and asked him to wake me up when chow was ready. I finally woke up the next morning—twenty-four hours later. The cook told me that he started to wake me, but Captain Woodside said to let me sleep.

We stayed in Niederweiller for several days of training and rest. On March 11, we left by truck at 0130 for Haute-Kontz, France where we spent the better part of the day cleaning up, shaving, and generally taking a one-day break from the front lines.

We returned north by truck to Saarburg on March 12, then marched four miles to near Oberzerf to begin preparations for a major attack the next day. This was to be a division-size maneuver.

Early on the morning of March 13, the 317th was to move out, pass through elements of the 26th Infantry Division, cross the Zerf River, and take the high ground east and southeast of Oberzerf. The 318th and 319th regiments had similar assignments, completing the division line of attack. In addition to support by division artillery, our regiment would have the 313th Field Artillery Battalion in support as well as a company from the 702nd Tank Battalion and a company from the 811th Tank Destroyer Battalion.

As we marched to our bivouac area in the afternoon, we passed through a long line of tanks that were double parked on each side of the road. Beyond our bivouac area was a long stretch of artillery.

The artillery opened fire in the early evening and continued all night long, but we were so accustomed to it that we were able to get a few hours of sleep.

Chapter 11
Wound Number Three
March 13, 1945–April 10, 1945

At 0200 on the morning of March 15, 1945, our battalion received orders to move up. As we advanced through the artillery, we were told that we would filter through the lines of the unit in front of us at 0400.

As soon as we moved out on schedule, the Germans started lobbing mortars at us. Mortar fragments travel up and out in an arc, so your chances of being hit are reduced if you are on the ground. When one round hit about twenty yards to our front, we all hit the deck.

As I was going down, another round landed about ten feet to my left. I felt something hit my forearm and left thigh, and assumed it was dirt clods. The Germans seldom shortened their range, so I ordered my men to move forward. When I tried to get up, I felt blood running down my arm, and I couldn't stand on my left leg. Those weren't dirt clods.

Although Marvin Glick was no longer my official bodyguard, he still kept an eye on me. I yelled, "Glick, I've been hit. I need some help." He and Baca ran up and helped me to my feet. They began to pull me back to the aid station while I tried to push them away, shouting to them that I just needed to get my bearings.

"Lieutenant, you've been hit and you need to get back to the aid station," said Glick.

"It's a minor wound. Get a medic up here and bandage it up so we can keep going," I replied.

"No, sir. We're getting you back to the aid station."

They had always obeyed my orders without question; their insistence was out of character. I was bleeding and in pain when they got me back to the aid station and found a medic, who attempted to give me morphine.

Ready-made vials of morphine with glass-encased needles, called syrettes, were used to ease pain. The medic tried in vain three times to give me an injection, but the syrettes wouldn't work. Though we were well into the month of March, the temperatures were still very cold at night, and moisture in the syrettes had frozen.

The pain level was rising. I conceded that I was pretty badly wounded and losing blood. I told Glick to write up an LWA (Lightly Wounded in Action) form, and then I waited for an ambulance to take me back to a field hospital.

I did not have to wait long. As soon as an ambulance showed up, four of us were loaded in. We rode for a few minutes and stopped a short distance from a road intersection. The ambulance driver told us that the Germans had artillery registered on this intersection, that he wanted to wait for the next round to land before he crossed. Sure enough, after a brief interval, a shell landed very close to the intersection. The driver navigated his way around numerous craters and sped on to the field hospital, which had been set up in an old schoolhouse several miles behind the lines.

I was checked in, and, as before, I told them they could have anything they wanted except my jacket and my boots. When I arrived, I had a wool muffler wrapped around my neck and a jacket that zipped all the way up to my chin. An orderly started to remove my clothes. He took off my field jacket, held it up to me and said, "Lieutenant, you're damn lucky." The zipper had been ripped away by shrapnel. My wool muffler had several holes in it, and the back of my field jacket had fourteen holes in it. I was not happy about the two wounds that I had sustained, but suffice it to say, it could have been worse.

As I was being attended to, I noticed quite a commotion on one of the tables near me. Several orderlies were holding a man down while a doctor worked on his neck. "What are they doing to that guy?" I asked.

"They're inserting a plastic tube in his trachea to try and save him, just like the article in the Stars and Stripes. They cannot put him to sleep."

There had been a recent article in Stars and Stripes, the newspaper for servicemen, about a front-line medic who took desperate measures to try to save a man who had been wounded and could not breathe. The medic made a crude incision in his throat, then took the barrel of a fountain pen, cleaned it with whiskey, and inserted it in into the wounded man's trachea. The medic's resourceful action saved the man's life. I think the man in the field hospital also pulled through.

The orderly, after removing my jacket and boots, got out a pair of scissors, started at the bottom of my pants, and cut off every stitch of clothing I had on. After that, I was put to sleep and the shrapnel in my leg and arm was removed. The fragment in my leg was about three inches long. The piece in my forearm was small, but it had embedded itself between the two bones. The next thing I knew, someone was placing a tray of food on my chest and saying, "Here's your supper."

The normal procedure for a wound like mine was to remove the shrapnel, stuff the wound with a Vaseline wick and wrap it. The wick would remain in place for a few days, after which the wound would be sewn up and the body's healing powers would take over.

A nurse woke me up the next morning with a somewhat alarmed look on her face. "You are as white as a sheet," she told me. My leg was bandaged and I was wearing a pair of pajamas. I was on a mattress that had been placed on a cot. There was a pool of blood on the floor; I had lost enough blood for it to soak through the mattress.

Orderlies were loading up men to be transferred to a hospital in Verdun, France. I don't think that the nature of my wound would normally have required a transfer, but I heard her say, "Get this one." I still had on my pajamas, which we were supposed to turn in if we left, but she told me to keep the covers on and to not say anything.

The facility in Verdun was a bona fide French hospital. I got settled in and began to recuperate, but my bad luck at hospitals continued. The staff focused on my arm, and neglected my leg. One day I asked a nurse when they were going to sew up the wound in my leg. She pulled the covers back, looked at it and said, "Omigosh," and immediately attended to it. A few days later they sewed it up and it began to heal.

In the quiet hospital environment, I became aware of a ringing in both of my ears that did not go away. In fact, it has been present ever since. That mortar round landed really close.

A few days after being admitted to the hospital, I received an interesting letter from Marvin Glick. I had acquired a really nice trench coat somewhere along the line, and when I went back to the aid station, I gave it to Glick and told him to take care of it for me. The purpose of his letter was to inform me that he had lost my prized coat. "But don't worry," he continued, "you are not the only one to lose something. General McBride was at regimental headquarters a few days ago and his jeep took a direct hit." The general was away from the jeep and wasn't injured.

That was a really nice coat.

**

While in the hospital, I became friends with another lieutenant, Bill Mooney. As we healed, we offered to help admit patients and take care of others not as far along as we were. We sort of got the cure from helping admit new patients when a man came in with an abdominal wound. We went over to see what was going on and peered over the nurse's shoulder. She carefully unwrapped the bandages from his abdomen to reveal his intestines, which were sitting on top of his stomach. All of the carnage I had witnessed on the battlefield did not ease my discomfort at seeing body parts in the wrong place. Our eagerness to help with admitting of new patients subsided considerably.

Another lieutenant named Kay Moore was admitted. He had been in an armored car when a round from a German tank scored a direct hit on the vehicle, splattering his whole backside with hundreds of tiny metal slivers. Also, a large chunk of skin was missing from his back. All he remembered, vaguely, was two men dragging him several blocks after he had been hit. He was taken to a field hospital, where the doctors did not expect him to live. He said that a nurse sat next to his bed for twenty-four hours, caring for him and encouraging him. He credited her for helping him to sustain the will to live. Many of the larger slivers had been removed at the field hospital before he was transferred, but he still had a lot of metal in him.

I watched one morning as a nurse painstakingly removed what had to have been a hundred slivers. Kay and I became close friends and I sort of took on the role of personal orderly to him. It took a long time for him to recuperate, but he finally got well enough to get out of bed and move around.

The 80th Moves On

The 80th Division, true to their motto, "Only Moves Forward," continued to push the Germans deeper into their homeland—with no assistance from me. In four days, from March 18 to 21, the division advanced one hundred and fifteen miles and took 5,084 prisoners along the way. Morale escalated as more and more enemy units surrendered.

Evidence of the state of the war was sometimes manifested in almost comical fashion.

At one point Able Company had just completed a clearing action in a small town and moved to an elevated plateau, somewhat sparsely wooded, and stopped briefly on the front edge of the plateau. Our men came under harassing small arms fire from a tree grove at the far end of the plateau, about a hundred and fifty yards away. They took cover and returned fire while a squad was dispatched around the perimeter of the area to at least recon the enemy troops, perhaps to attack their flank. Within a few minutes, as soon as the squad opened fire from the flank, the rest of the company saw German soldiers literally rise to their feet and run over and down the back slope of the plateau. The whole company spontaneously rose to its feet, yelling war whoops, and chased the Germans off of the ridge.

At the bottom of the ridge was a small creek. Ed Sprunger found himself chasing a German soldier who was unable to keep up with the rest. Ed was gaining on him when the man fell to the ground near the stream. Sprunger, who had arrived in the theater a mere five days earlier, was about fifty feet behind and not sure how to respond to this strange behavior. Impulsively, he mimicked his foe and dropped to the ground as well. Both men lay motionless, feigning injury, but knowing the other was pretending. Each man waited to see what the other would do. It was almost a game. The German lay still until the company had passed, looked around, slowly got to his feet, and began to run again. Sprunger stayed down until the man was almost out of sight, jumped up, and ran to catch up with the rest of the company. Neither man fired a shot or even made a hostile move.

**

An order was issued On March 26 to prepare for the crossing of the Rhine River at its juncture with the Mainz. The Rhine was an almost sacred boundary to the Germans, so the crossing carried much more meaning than crossing any other river. This was to be a significant event.

At 0100 on March 28, the 2nd Battalion, 317th Infantry Regiment, jumped off. Navy personnel had been brought in to transport the division in large assault boats. Over the strong protests of Major James Hayes, who was now regimental operations officer, General McBride ordered that the crossing be made with no preparatory artillery support. Major Hayes had seen indications that the Germans on the opposite bank were inexperienced and tentative, and he concluded that the benefits of a heavy artillery barrage would easily outweigh anything gained by attempting a surprise attack. The skies were clear and the moon was bright, so there would actually be no element of surprise.

Major Hayes was correct. The enemy was able to observe every phase of the preparations to cross the river. As the first wave of assault boats loaded out troops and lined up to launch, it must have been a forward observer's dream. He called in spotting rounds and radioed back to fire for effect, bringing a deadly barrage into the defenseless group.

The navy lieutenant leading the crossing was killed before he pushed off. The initial wave suffered more than two hundred casualties, and a number of the officers in 2nd Battalion were killed or wounded. Major Hayes's assessment of the enemy was further bolstered when, as soon as American troops began to land on the opposite shore, German soldiers abandoned their guns and surrendered en masse.

The spoils of the successful but costly crossing were the treasures of Wiesbaden and surrounding villages, which included an airplane factory, an airfield, six enemy aircraft, an ordnance repair depot with lots of ammunition, and a champagne factory

135

stocked with four thousand *cases* of champagne. The men helped themselves to souvenir weapons and all of the bubbly they could carry. Spirits were reportedly pretty high for the next few days.

Kassel

The 80th Infantry Division traveled north from Wiesbaden by truck on the autobahn all day on March 31, covering a distance of more than a hundred miles. The couple of days at Wiesbaden had been quiet, but everyone knew that things would heat up as they moved further into Germany. The next objective for the division was the city of Kassel. The 318th and 319th regiments would lead the assault with the 317th in reserve.

April 1—Easter Sunday—found Able Company stationed in the sleepy little town of Linsingen, situated in an open area just outside of Kassel, with woods to the east and north. The men were billeted in houses in town. Following the usual procedure, the German occupants were given fifteen minutes to vacate their homes, or sometimes be confined to the basement. The outposts had detected enemy movements in the woods to the north during the night, so Pfc Ed Sprunger and two other men were sent to conduct a recon in the early morning. Each man was armed with a BAR.

They moved out to the east into the woods, almost the opposite direction of the suspected enemy position, and circled in a clockwise direction, skirting the woods with the intention of coming up behind the Germans.

After twenty minutes and several hundred yards, they detected movement and heard voices. They slowly crept forward until they could see what appeared to be almost a platoon of Germans, loosely deployed. Amazingly, all the Germans faced the town; not a single soldier guarded their rear.

Sprunger and his other two patrol members conferred, and agreed that, though they were greatly outnumbered, they had the element of surprise *and* automatic weapons. Rather than backtrack to the village and report what they had seen, they felt the odds were good that they could overpower this whole troop. They spread out about twenty yards apart and moved to within fifty feet. On Ed's signal, all three fired a burst into the air. Startled Germans whirled around or dropped to the ground. "Drop your weapons and put your hands in the air," yelled Sprunger.

The enemy troops were caught flatfooted. They did not know that they were facing only three GIs, but none was inclined to take any heroic action to test assumptions. All quickly surrendered without a fight. The three men lined them up and made sure they discarded their weapons, noting that most of the thirty men they captured were armed with American .45-caliber pistols. Ed and the others marched the Germans single-file down the slope out of the woods, and into Linsengen, from which they were sent back to the rear to join other POWs.

The Germans had been in a perfect position to ambush the town from the American left flank. They were too few in number to have won a battle, but they could have executed a hit-and-run tactic and inflicted serious casualties.

The battle for Kassel and the surrounding territory lasted five days. Our men were surprised by the number of tanks they encountered, especially heavy Tiger tanks. It seemed that every time they knocked one out, another appeared. After taking the town, they discovered a Tiger tank factory hidden in the side of a hill on the outskirts. A tank training facility was about fifty miles away, so fresh crews moved in, manned the tanks, and engaged.

**

As the Allied forces bored further into the Rhineland, captured German soldiers consistently stated the obvious: they had no chance of winning, and the every-day soldier was ready to pack it in and go home to be with his family. As a fighting force, however, the Wehrmacht continued to send deadly barrages of artillery and mortars, and it mounted seemingly random counterattacks, usually followed by withdrawal.

Although the men of the 80th were exhausted, war-weary, and eager to go home, their resolve to finish strong and punish the enemy was reinforced as various units began to come upon concentration camps. Combat-hardened veterans were overcome with nausea and deep emotion upon seeing the emaciated bodies of the living and the dead, who had suffered such inhumane treatment at the hands of their captors. They did what they could to feed and relieve the suffering of the survivors, but the cruelty inflicted on fellow human beings by the Nazis was beyond what our soldiers could imagine, in spite of the brutality of combat they had experienced thus far. Their mission was to move forward, so they stayed until other units could come in that were better qualified for this kind of duty.

The next targets were Gotha, Erfurt, Weimar, and Jena. Gotha did not offer much resistance, but the Germans mounted a strong defense in the Erfurt area.

The 2nd Battalion moved east on April 10 against small arms fire, through Tottlestadt and Salomensborn and into the towns of Kiliani and Gispersleben. The 1st Battalion, following in reserve to the southwest, moved into Salomensborn.

The terrain consisted of gentle rolling hills interspersed with patches of forest. The company dug in just to the east of one of these wooded areas, with a slope of clear ground rising up behind them.

Dusk was approaching. Sergeant Guy Furgiuele, a squad leader in 2nd Platoon, was hoping for some hot chow when an American tank with a rocket launcher mounted on it pulled up behind him. The crew dismounted and loaded about a hundred small rockets into the launcher. They climbed back into the tank and fired the rockets in sequence while the troops looked on in amazement. The launching of the entire sheaf took only thirty seconds, after which the tank beat a hasty retreat over the hill to the rear. The men were still shaking their heads when Furgiuele looked up and realized that the cloud of smoke hovering above them was equivalent to a neon sign to the Germans, imploring them to send over artillery shells.

"Get the hell out of here," he yelled at his men.

The troops grabbed their rifles and scrambled up the hillside, running for the safety of the back side of the hill, but the Germans were too quick for them. Before the squad could get to the crest, the whole area erupted with exploding artillery and mortar rounds.

A replacement who had joined Furgiuele's squad a few days earlier went down. Furgiuele crawled over to see if he could help the man, but before he could do anything, a mortar round landed at the wounded man's feet, blowing both of his legs off. Both men screamed for a medic, but there was none to be seen. Furgiuele lay next to the wounded man, hoping and praying that he would survive. Finally, after the barrage ended and darkness was setting in, a medic showed up. He gave the man a shot of morphine and wrapped up what was left of his legs to stop the bleeding. Furgiuele and the medic wrapped him in a blanket, put him on a stretcher, and carried him a hundred yards to a jeep to be transported to a clearing station. He had lost a lot of blood and was in shock, but he was alive.

Furgiuele was also in shock. Unable to stop shaking, he found a place to be alone to try and calm down. He was angry—angry at himself for not remembering the man's name or hometown; angry at the darkness that must reside in mankind to produce so much destruction and death; angry at God for letting it happen. He was at a breaking point.

He finally got to his feet and found his platoon. Having lost his foxhole buddy, Pete Nicola, a few days before to a neck wound in the battle for Kassel, he endured a sleepless, tormented night in his foxhole, all alone. He never found out whether the man lived or not.

Chapter 12
Surprise Attack
April 10, 1945–April 12, 1945

Able Company spent the night spread out from Salomensborn southward to near the Erfurt airport. The towns were geographically in an equilateral triangle configuration with Salomensborn and Erfurt at the bottom and Kiliani at the peak. The village of Marbach was in the middle of the triangle.

At 0500 on the morning of April 11, Able Company moved out with the rest of the battalion to undertake the two-mile march northeast to relieve 2nd Battalion.

There was light early morning fog, but by all indications it was going to be a nice spring day. They were in farm country now—gently rolling hills of mostly plowed ground with scattered farm houses and an occasional row of trees lining the roads.

The regiment had just received an influx of replacements—108 men on the April 6 and 153 on the 9th. Their only experience with live ammunition had been on the firing range and a few live-fire maneuvers in Stateside training. They were assimilated into various companies and platoons. As they marched, they peppered the experienced men with questions about what to expect in a fire fight and how to respond if they were to come under attack.

The battalion moved along with the men in 3rd Platoon, A Company, on the right flank of the formation, traveling north along a road near the Erfurt airport. As the fog burned off, the troops could see tanks in the distance to their right and moving parallel to them. The veterans took comfort in the assumption that the tanks were part of the 4th Armored Division, which had provided dependable support since their arrival on the Continent.

Sergeant Furgiuele was marching along the dusty road, still trying to cope with the events of the previous evening. He wondered if the wounded man was still alive and how many more limbs he would see blown off before the war ended. As the sun came up, he became aware that his fatigues were stiff from the wounded man's dried blood. He threw off his field jacket and poured canteen water on his hands to wash off the blood.

The tranquility of the morning was snapped as the "friendly" tanks in the distance rotated their turrets 90 degrees to the left and opened fire on the American troops. They then turned to make a frontal attack, with scores of infantrymen in trail using the tanks for cover, firing as they moved.

The air was filled with German ordnance and the cries of men. Several of our men fell in the first volley. Seasoned troops yelled at the new guys to get down or find cover. Men cried out in panic or pain. Every man who was able headed for the nearest farm house on the double.

GIs stormed into houses, sheds, barns, or any other structure that was close and could provide any protection whatsoever. Terrified German families stayed out of the way as the American troops burst into their homes and either sought out hiding places or set up firing positions.

As soon as the tanks opened fire, Sergeant Furgiuele and two men in his squad sprinted to a nearby house. They burst through the door and found a middle-aged lady present. Quickly and emphatically bridging the language gap, they communicated that she was not to divulge their whereabouts to any German soldiers. They scampered down to the basement, found hiding places, and waited. Within a few minutes, they heard the front door open, followed by a very animated discussion in German. After a slight pause, they heard the click of hobnail boots walking across the wooden floor above them.

The basement door swung open.

"Okay, you GIs come out with your hands up, or we will drop a cannon shell in your lap."

Silence.

Had the lady betrayed them? Had she been coerced? Were the Germans going to come down the stairs and shoot the place up? If so, the Americans were doomed.

No one moved.

The door closed.

She must not have told them.

The men could hear another brief conversation, after which the German soldiers departed. Furgiuele and his men stayed in place for another hour and a half before they heard American voices outside sounding the all-clear and calling for any GIs in the house to come out. The men ran up the stairs and each planted a kiss on the lady's cheek as they exited.

**

Herb Barwell, a replacement who had joined Able Company in late February, was platoon sergeant of 1st Platoon. He and a couple of other men took refuge in the first structure they could find, which was a teepee-shaped stand of wooden stakes, used by the Germans to help grow vegetables. Peering through the gaps in the stakes, they could see the battle unfold, as tanks and tank destroyers from the 4th Armored Division engaged the German panzers.

Nothing had changed regarding the use of an M1 against an armored vehicle. This was essentially a tank battle, which left the infantrymen little option but to stay out of the line of fire and hope for the 4th Armored Division to overpower the Germans. In Barwell's case, they were never spotted nor seriously threatened by enemy soldiers. They waited out the storm, and when it was over, came out of their hiding place to join in alerting soldiers in other houses that the Germans had been repulsed.

Barwell had seen men fall when the attack began, but he didn't realize how many casualties there were, especially Germans, until he was able to survey the surrounding farmland. Motionless bodies lay scattered in every direction.

**

Ray Patterson and part of his squad ran through the back door of the house nearest them, and up the stairs, opting for a good vantage point from which to see what was happening. The startled residents huddled together in a corner of the first floor.

German soldiers moved past the house, some using it for cover against America fire, but none came into the house. At one point, Patterson had a good shot at an enemy soldier hiding behind a chicken coop with his lower extremities exposed. Considering the attention it might bring, he held his fire and watched as the man eventually got to his feet and moved on. They watched with relief as tanks from the 4th Armored Division appeared and drove the German tanks back towards Erfurt.

**

As Jerry Balach's squad came up over a small knoll the village of Marbach came into view. The town appeared a little too peaceful, so the men spread out and approached warily. Jerry was a bazooka man from Headquarters Company, but since there was a shortage of bazookas, he had been issued an M1 and temporarily assigned to a rifle squad. Though he was tired from standing guard duty the night before, the sound of gunfire off in the distance brought his senses to full alert.

As the squad cautiously approached the first few houses, the whole village exploded. Concealed enemy troops opened fire on the left while tanks pulled out from between houses on the right. It was an ambush.

Jerry was knocked to the ground as shrapnel from an 88mm round penetrated his left thigh. Unable to stand, he called for help. Two of his buddies grabbed him and pulled him into the first house they could reach, then half carried and half dragged him down to the basement. They gave him first aid, then ran up the stairs and returned fire. Jerry lay still, wondering what he would do if the Germans raided the house. He would not be able to defend himself. All he could do was wait.

Finally he heard the men begin to cheer as the tank destroyers moved in and the German tanks retreated. Shortly, the medics arrived and put him on a stretcher and strapped it onto the side of a jeep. His buddies congratulated him as he left. For him, the war was over.

**

Ed Sprunger and his buddy, Fred Moneysmith, were spotted as they sprinted into a home where they drew fire. Their presence made the house an obvious target, and with rounds ricocheting off of the walls, they looked for somewhere else to hide. In desperation, they ran out the back door and took refuge in a wooden shed behind the house, but a German tanker saw them as they darted across the open space. Ed, who instinctively wanted to open fire on the tank, started to raise his rifle, but Fred grabbed him and yanked him to the floor.

"Get down, and stay down," yelled Moneysmith.

The tank opened up with its machine gun. The two men lay flat on the floor as rounds slammed into the small building and sent chunks of wood, splinters, and glass flying in every direction. The German gunner raked back and forth across the building as the Americans lay motionless, hoping he would not lower the barrel to floor level and make another pass. It was a surreal, terrifying few moments, made more so by the fact that both men had been with the unit for fewer than thirty days.

The firing stopped.

It was eerily silent. Dust floated in the air.

The two men held their breath.

Were they alone? Surrounded? They could hear the sounds of battle close by. Should they stay on the floor? Was it safe to move? Were German soldiers waiting outside to finish them off?

Sprunger spoke first. "We have to surrender," he declared. "They know we're here and they're going to kill us."

"The hell we are. Just stay put."

They heard the sound of the tank engine revving up and then fading away.

"Okay, here's what we are going to do," said Moneysmith. "The house is safer than this place. When I say 'Go,' we're going back in."

"GO!"

They sprinted to the house and through the back door, this time drawing no fire. Two middle-aged ladies were inside, scared but composed. German soldiers were setting up defensive positions outside of the house on three sides: machine guns in front and one side, and a couple of men on the third side hiding behind some bushes, potato masher grenades in hand, watching for targets of opportunity in the adjacent orchard.

Sprunger and Moneysmith had been issued K-rations that morning, so they quickly handed the meals over to the ladies with strict instructions: "No Americans in the house." The women nodded, and the men tore down the stairs to the basement. Moneysmith hid in the coal bin while Sprunger hid in a closet.

The pair hunkered down while the battle raged outside. Eventually, the machine gun fire subsided and they heard talking and hobnail boots above. No one came downstairs.

The sound of battle faded, but the men dared not move. Finally, one of the ladies opened the basement door and announced, "American panzers coming. American panzers coming."

The men cautiously emerged from their hiding places and went upstairs. Sure enough, American tanks were traveling across the fields where the Germans had been a couple of hours earlier.

As they walked outside, Sprunger was surprised by the number of dead German soldiers in the area, especially in the orchard. He walked over to one young man, rolled him over and searched his pockets. In a breast pocket was a picture of the soldier with his wife and son. It was a family portrait, somewhat wrinkled and frayed, not unlike the ones that lined the pockets of many of Ed's buddies. An unexpected wave of sadness took him off guard as he studied the photograph. This young man's family would never see him again; they would grieve his loss and try to move on, just as would thousands of American wives and sons. Perhaps, when all was said and done, he and his anonymous adversary were not really so different.

**

Pfc Justin Baca had been driving a jeep, pulling a small trailer loaded with ammunition and a couple of machine guns. When the attack began, he immediately pulled off of the road and parked behind a house. He, along with three buddies—Sergeant Larkin, Sergeant Schroeder, and Staff Sergeant Knight—and seventeen other men, charged through the back door. Most of the seventeen were replacements who had just arrived. They quickly unloaded their gear and set up the machine guns to fire out of the windows at ground level in the basement. An old man and a teenage girl, the only occupants, huddled together in a corner of the basement, crying softly.

A few days before, Baca and his three buddies, well aware that they had, so far, beaten the odds by surviving eight months of combat, stacked hands and made a pact that they would never surrender under any circumstances.

The Germans moved toward the farmhouse with tanks and foot troops, firing as they approached, although the tanks, probably deferring to the civilian occupants, checked fire on their main turret guns. Some of the men in Baca's group returned fire, but it quickly became apparent that they were outgunned and outmanned.

A grenade came through the window and went off, tearing into Sergeant Shroeder's right foot. The grenade and the sight of German troops approaching and firing into the house threw the recruits into a panic. They refused to man the weapons, and begged loudly for the experienced men to stop shooting and surrender. As the shouting and arguing intensified, a German Panzer IV tank pulled up to the house. It stopped ten feet from a basement window. The barrel lowered to an angle pointing directly into the window, and the tank commander stood up in the turret.

"All right, you guys, are you going to surrender, or am I going to have to blow your heads off?" he asked, addressing them in flawless English.

Sergeant Knight volunteered to run up to the second story and drop a hand grenade into the turret opening, which sent the recruits into further hysteria.

"In case you are wondering about my English, my dad was a consul in Ohio, and I went to school in Cleveland. By the way, I'm a Red Sox fan. How are they doing this year?"

No one knew nor cared about the Red Sox at this point.

"You know that you are going to lose the war. Why don't you surrender to us?" countered Sergeant Knight.

"The war is not over, and I have no plans to surrender. I will give you one more chance—come out with your hands up or I will blow this house to pieces. Do what I say and, who knows, maybe someday we will all sit down and have a beer together."

The only option that made sense was to surrender, so the men laid down their weapons and filed out of the house. The four veterans, angry and humbled at so quickly reneging on their solemn pledge, mumbled to each other under their breath, and quietly agreed to escape at the first opportunity, even if the odds for success were slim.

The tank commander assigned the POWs to some infantry soldiers and they trekked across a plowed field. They were about halfway across the field when Charlie Company, located in a tree line about a thousand yards away, opened fire on the whole group.

As the German guards returned fire, Baca yelled, *"NOW!"*

The four veterans each took off in a different direction, including Shroeder, who, with the help of a shot of adrenalin was able to hobble away. Following a brief exchange of gunfire with Charlie Company, the guards turned their rifles on the four escapees. All four hit the deck, but only Baca was hit; a bullet grazed his left forearm. The replacement troops huddled together like sheep and were hustled the rest of the way to enemy lines.

The four veterans lay motionless in furrows for some time while the battle steadily moved away. After what seemed like at least an hour and a half, a patrol from Charlie Company approached and escorted them back to their unit, where Baca and Schroeder were sent to the clearing station for treatment of their wounds.

The company regrouped and continued on to Kiliani and Gispersleben as the Germans retreated back to Erfurt. The next morning, the whole battalion pressed the attack into Erfurt, where it captured several hundred prisoners and secured the release of the seventeen Able Company men who had been captured.

Chapter 13
The Final Days
April 12, 1945–May 8, 1945

As the division moved further into Germany, not only did German soldiers defect in large numbers, but more and more of them left the ranks of their units and simply went back to their home towns. Sergeant Patterson told me of one instance in a small town they swept in late April where he was given charge over a German officer and enlisted man. Ray was escorting them back to a POW processing center when the officer stopped in front of a house, pointed upstairs, and said "Frau."

"What the hell are you talking about?" Ray responded. "No Frau." The German cobbled together enough English words to communicate to Ray that he wanted to say goodbye to his wife. He was of medium build, had sandy blonde hair, and certainly was not combative. Ray noticed he was wearing a nice looking watch.

"Hand over the watch and you can go see your Frau," he said, pointing to the timepiece. "I'll give you twenty minutes." The officer removed the watch, handed it over, and went into the house. Patterson and his enlisted prisoner waited outside as GIs and an occasional German citizen walked by, the latter either avoiding eye contact or glancing warily at Ray, who had his M1 rifle slung over his shoulder. Children stared with fascination as they walked by with their parents. The mood in the town was that the war was unofficially over. People were weary and ready to concede and begin rebuilding their lives.

The house was small but neat, with a few flowers out front, a fence around the tiny yard, and a small gate in front. As Ray waited, he couldn't help but reflect on the similarities between the American and German cultures and lifestyles. Many of the U.S. servicemen were surprised that the small towns, their layout, family lifestyles, and standard of living were more similar to the

148

American way of life than the Allied countries they had been through.

Twenty minutes later, almost to the minute, the officer appeared at the doorway. He gave his wife a goodbye kiss and walked through the gate. Had Ray not lost so many buddies to men wearing the uniform of his prisoners, he might have felt a touch of sentimentality, but he did not let himself go there.

It was customary for the German officers to maintain an aloofness from, even disdain, for their enlisted men, so Ray was surprised when the officer opened a sack with two sandwiches and gave one to his fellow soldier. The trio continued on to battalion headquarters, where Ray turned in his prisoners.

The War Ends

I was still in the hospital when we got word of VE day—May 8, 1945. The sense of joy and relief we felt is difficult to convey. A celebration was in order. We sent someone to the PX to buy beer and ended up with about a gallon and a half to split among several of us, including my buddy Kay Moore. As the beer was consumed, spirits rose and inhibitions fell. Several of the men got somewhat carried away, and the next thing I knew, Kay was out in the middle of the floor dancing. Our celebration eventually subsided and Kay did not get out of bed for three days.

Return to my Unit; June 1945

I returned to my unit around the first of June. The war in Europe was over, and the reality of that fact was sinking in with all of us. We all wanted to go home, but there was a sense of relief that we had survived.

Able Company had landed in early August 1944. The rumor mill had it that we had experienced a 600 percent casualty rate. With occasional recording errors and men being wounded and returning, some more than once, confirming the accuracy of such a statistic would be a very difficult, especially inasmuch as those records are not usually compiled at a company level. Suffice it to say that we lost a lot of men.

Chapter 14
Occupation
May 8, 1945–November 21, 1945

When I returned, my unit was stationed in an old German barracks in downtown Garmisch-Partinkirshen, just north of the Austrian border. It had been a German playground before the war and was gorgeous country. We could look in any direction and see snow-capped mountains. There were a number of scenic lakes in the area, all of which were crystal clear. You could go out in a boat and see fish clearly twenty feet down.

Everything was very clean and orderly. It was not uncommon to see a house two or three hundred years old, and some had concrete walls six to eight inches thick.

We had very little fraternization with the Germans, and that suited both sides fine. The everyday civilians were dispirited, beaten down, and nearly impoverished. They had little in the way of material possessions or even food. There were stores and shops, but, no matter what their wares, shelves were all but bare. Some of the German women foraged through our garbage for food. It was probably against a regulation somewhere, but we looked the other way.

We stayed there for about four months. Things were lax, somewhat boring, actually. Men relaxed by playing sports and going to the USO club to hang out. We also watched movies or enjoyed a performance by traveling USO entertainers.

After we moved into our barracks, we began training for the invasion of Japan, but the training was not very intense. We did not engage in large-scale field maneuvers, but we did take part in smaller exercises and courses, such as how to use a compass and call artillery. I remember one exercise where I boarded a Piper Cub with the battalion forward observer. We flew over a group of men and dropped simulated bombs on them. The bombs were sacks of flour.

When the Japanese emperor announced his surrender on August 15, we breathed a sigh of relief.

Czechoslovakia, September 1945

From Southern Germany, we were transferred to Tremosna, Czechoslovakia, in the eastern region of Plzen. It was a town of about five hundred houses, only two of which had running water. We were billeted in homes with the local population. Many families kept one or two soldiers in their homes. They had been an occupied country and were glad to see us.

When we first got there, we relieved an artillery battalion. In talking to the battery commander, I found out that we had come in on the tail end of some interesting developments. Things were calming down from a standoff with the Soviets, who had occupied the place before our artillery unit had arrived. American troops occupied the town and surrounding area and the Russians had stopped their advance right next to the Americans. The two forces were in close quarters—too close. The American and Russian commanders had a meeting and agreed that each force would move back a half a kilometer, giving them a one-kilometer free zone. The Americans moved back the agreed on half kilometer, and when they awoke up the next morning, the Russians were right next to them.

General Patton, who was still in command of Third Army, immediately sent three of our combat divisions into the area. They set up artillery and machine gun emplacements and got ready to do battle. The Soviets realized they were not going to be able to bully Patton, so they pulled back to the agreed one kilometer. A contingent of about five hundred men stayed for awhile longer to make sure the Russians didn't make another attempt at poaching.

The homes in Tremosna, even though they did not have running water, had indoor toilets. I was company commander again when our regimental commander gave us instructions to build some outdoor latrines. I talked to the local mayor about our intentions and was told that we would have to get permission from Prague, the capital of Czechoslovakia, for a project like that.

While we were stuck on this point, a corps commander came through on an inspection tour. He asked me about the latrine project and I explained where we were in the process. "What?" he asked. "Do you mean we have to get permission from Prague to build a shithouse?"

As with most generals, he had an entourage. As we talked, he put a cigarette in his mouth, pulled a lighter out of his pocket, and started flicking it to light the cigarette. After a few flicks, he gave up and tossed the lighter over his shoulder. A lieutenant had stationed himself at precisely the right place to catch the lighter, and a private first class stepped up as if on cue and lit the general's cigarette with a match. It was too well choreographed to have been the first time this had happened.

We were transferred before the outhouse issue was resolved.

**

While we were in Tremosna, we had an outbreak of trench mouth. It was bad enough that the medical guys decided to see what was causing the problem. A medic was sent over to try to figure out the cause. Each man had his own mess kit. After eating, they washed and dried their own dishes. The medic determined that the drying step was the root of the problem. We needed to let our utensils drip dry. When I explained to him that rust would form on the utensils, he replied that rust was not going to be a problem; if we let the utensils air dry, the trench mouth would go away. I disagreed but followed his instructions anyway. He was right. Within a few days, our trench mouth problem went away.

Epilogue; 80th Division

By the end of the war, May 7, 1945, the 80th Infantry Division had seen 277 days of combat. We had captured 212,295 enemy soldiers.

The division returned to the United States in January 1946, after spending time in Europe helping to restore and maintain peace and order after the war. Our division had been a stalwart of Patton's Third Army, but at a heavy cost. We had 17,087 casualties:

Killed in Action	3038
Wounded	12,484
Missing	488
Captured	1,077
Total Casualties	17,087

According to reports, the 80th Division's "bloodiest day" was October 8, 1944, where approximately one hundred and fifteen men lost their lives. The "bloodiest month" was September 1944.

Winding Down, November 1945

By now, the army's efforts to return the troops home were bearing fruit, which, to no one's surprise, resulted in confusion and uncertainty. Unit integrity dissolved and men from infantry units were mixed with artillery and armor units in preparation for return to the States. At one point, my company was moved to an old wooden German barracks and I was told to report to corps headquarters. I reported to a colonel, who handed me a manual on camp management and informed me that I was now the camp commander.

It was cold enough that we had wood-burning stoves going all night in the barracks. My first concern was for fire safety, so I had someone make up a duty roster for night fire watch.

A week later, I was again summoned to the colonel's office. I reported as instructed, not knowing what he had in mind. I waited for him to speak. "Lieutenant," he said, "would you like to go home?" I could hardly believe my ears, nor could I believe that he would ask such a question. Keeping it simple, I answered in the affirmative. "You will be receiving orders shortly."

Finally the day I had been waiting for was in sight.

Chapter 15
Coming Home
November 21, 1945–December 14, 1945

My orders showed up as the colonel had promised. I packed my gear and was transported to a staging area in Germany. From there I boarded a 40 and 8 and traveled for three days to the coastal city of Marseille, France, where I boarded a Liberty ship bound for the U.S.

The trip over on the Queen Mary had been made at 30 knots, placing us in France after eight days of travel. This ship could make only 8 knots, extending our travel time to eighteen days.

The captain was drunk about half the time. At one point he was sure he had seen another ship in distress. We circled around for several hours and never saw anything.

When we were about six hundred miles from the East Coast, we ran into a violent storm that lasted forty-eight hours. The mess tables had a ridge around them, but at one point the ship listed so far over that everything on the tables spilled onto the floor. The only way we could stay in our bunks at night was to lay spread eagle on either our back or stomach. One of the crewmen told me the ship listed forty-three degrees at one time. By this time I had my sea legs and did not get sick.

We landed at Newport News, Virginia, in early December. One of the first things I did, along with several friends I had made on the trip, was to go directly to the PX, where we each bought a quart of cold milk and drank it down. I had never been very fond of milk, but it sure tasted good that day. That night for supper, everyone who had come in on the ship was served a steak dinner, which was quite a treat. There was one other thing that I had never had an appetite for and that was lettuce-and-tomato salad, but coming home, it took me about a year to get my fill of salad.

We stayed in Newport for a couple of days and then boarded trains for Camp Fannin in Tyler, Texas, where we would be mustered out. Following an uneventful two-day train ride, we ended up in Camp Fannin and were led to a large room with a lot of clerical people, each sitting at a desk. I was sitting in a waiting area, talking with someone, when I realized that all of the clerks had left the room. I asked what was happening and was told that it was break time. I had never been in a situation where people took coffee breaks.

One of the decisions we had to make in our out-processing was our future military status. My shipmate, Lieutenant Hibbert, and I had discussed this at length on the ship and agreed that if we became embroiled in another war, it would be with Russia, and every able-bodied man would be required to report for duty. Therefore, the prudent thing to do was to sign up for Inactive Reserve to maintain our present rank and seniority so that, in the event we were called up, we would not have to start over. I signed up for five years of Inactive Reserve, which almost got me into another war.

When all of our processing was completed, several of us hired a man to drive us to the bus station in Ft. Worth. We each chipped in $11.00. From there, I boarded a bus bound for Lubbock, about three hundred miles to the west, with one bus change in Wichita Falls. After changing buses in Wichita Falls, I sat down next to a man who patiently listened as I unloaded on him for the duration of the two-hour trip to Lubbock.

"I guess I talked your ear off," I said, as we pulled into the station in Lubbock.

"Don't worry about it," he replied. "I went through the same thing about three months ago."

West Texas in early December is cold, flat, and devoid of any vegetation, but, on this trip, I don't think Paradise itself would have been a more welcome sight. I was almost home.

Back to the Farm

I had written to Marie to let her know the approximate time I would arrive. I got my gear and took a cab to the house in which she lived. I walked up the sidewalk and knocked on the door. A lady answered, but it was not Marie. "Is Marie Adkisson here"? I asked.

"No, she moved. Here is her new address," the lady replied.

I got back into the cab and, following a short drive to the new address, again walked up the sidewalk and knocked on the door. This time no stranger answered the door. Marie was happy to see me, but her greeting was not exactly enthusiastic. Her hair was full of curlers, and I will never forget her first words: "I wasn't expecting you so soon." She wanted to look her best for me, which I appreciated, but curlers or not, she looked great to me. I was back in West Texas, with the woman I loved. Everything else was details.

I had yet to see my almost-one-year-old son, who was with Marie's folks in Quitaque, about ninety miles to the north. I was eager to see him, but we had to make one other stop before beginning my long-awaited stint as a dad. I wanted to go home. My older brother Douglas and his wife Thelma lived in Lubbock, which is about fifteen miles south of Abernathy. I called him and asked if he could take us to the farm the next day, which he was happy to do. My parents knew we were coming, but they did not know what time. I am the youngest of five children, but my two brothers were too old to be drafted, so I was the only member of the family serving.

The effects of winter on a West Texas farm are not pretty. The sky is usually clear, and the flat, sandy loam soil stretches as far as the eye can see, broken up only by occasional fields of unpicked cotton and clusters of barren trees surrounding farm houses a half mile apart. On this December day, none of this mattered. I would not have traded one square foot of this flat farmland for all of the forests, lakes, streams, or snow-capped mountains in all of Europe. I was home. I could hardly believe, as we turned down the half-mile dirt road that lad to the white stucco house that I was coming back in one piece after being away for two years.

My mother was beside herself as tears of joy flowed freely down her cheeks. My father, a dignified and somewhat reserved man, made it plain that he was glad to have me back home, safe and sound, but, whatever he was feeling, did not display much emotion. My mother prepared a special meal, and we sat down to eat and talk for a couple of hours.

We spent the night there and borrowed the car the next day to drive to Quitaque to bring our son home to stay. My mother was right, he was the spitting image of me. He was a happy baby and quickly adapted to having a full-time dad around as well as to his new surroundings.

Our plan was to take over the farm (the home place) and my parents' home. The folks would move into town, which they did within a few months, and I would get on with my life. When I left home, we had just purchased a crude, early generation tractor. Designs had advanced substantially during the war years and the new models were much in demand. Returning veterans were given first priority, so I wasted little time in acquiring the most popular brand and model. I bought a Farmall F-20, sporting a 20-horsepower engine and four gears, and it was able to pull a two-bottom plow. I felt like I was in "hog heaven."

It took some time to adjust to a tranquil, civilian life, but I was grateful to be back home in one piece and was ever mindful that many were not as fortunate as I. There is nothing like nine months in a war zone, in mostly miserable conditions, to put into perspective the blessings of a peaceful life, surrounded by family, with hot meals and a warm bed to sleep in every night. Planting cotton, taking care of the livestock, home-cooked meals, and a growing family were made richer against the backdrop of my time away from these things that I had once more or less taken for granted.

**

Our family grew as we welcomed another son and then a daughter. Things were going along swimmingly until 1950, when world developments almost brought an end to this good life. One month before my Army Reserve commitment was fulfilled, the U.S. government extended all reservist obligations indefinitely. Instead of my prediction that we would end up at war with Russia, we were preparing to send thousands of troops to Korea, and I was called up to report for a physical.

I reported as ordered to Reese Air Force Base in Lubbock. In a flashback to earlier days, I entered a room where dozens of men were filling out paperwork in preparation for a physical exam. It was common knowledge that war drums were sounding, but I wanted to find out a little more about how realistic my chances were of being back in uniform. I approached an Air Force sergeant

157

who seemed to know what was going on and, after a brief introduction, asked him my question.

"Sergeant," I said, "Are we going through a meaningless drill here, or am I looking at the possibility of traipsing around Korea with an M1?"

"Well, sir, this is as real as it gets. It looks like, in the next few months, we are going to be sending thousands of troops over. I see that you have already done your time in one war. This is going to be ugly, and I don't think you want any part of it."

I dutifully filled out my quota of forms, turned them in, and submitted to a typically thorough military physical. By that time, I was suffering from some pretty serious allergy and sinus problems, which were noted and discussed, after which I returned home to await the results. After an uneasy few days, I received a letter notifying me that I had flunked the physical, and was no longer qualified for active duty. That was one test that I had no regrets about failing.

Chapter 16
While I Was Away: Marie's Story
September 1, 1941–December 14, 1945

At the time Gid and I met, I was attending Texas Tech College in Lubbock, working toward a liberal arts degree. I was the next-to-youngest in a farm family with seven boys and two girls. Three of my older brothers were attending Tech at the time I entered school, and with my parents working hard just to make ends meet, my brothers and I were on our own financially. My older sister had already earned her degree from Tech, and gave me names of people with whom she had boarded when she was in school. I followed her lead and, in a very short time, was made welcome by two very nice families, the Helwigs and the McAffees. As it turned out, I ended up living with each family at different times.

Mr. Helwig was from Russia; he was a professor at Tech. His wife was French and loved to play golf. She was on the course at every opportunity. They had a three-year-old daughter named Annette, a sweet little girl whom I grew especially fond of, and after whom we later named our first daughter. I was provided room and board in exchange for taking care of Annette and doing cleaning and housework when I was not in class or working.

The McAffees were also very nice people. As with the Helwigs, I exchanged room and board for taking care of their children and helping with household chores. I fixed breakfast for the family in the morning, attended class until noon, had lunch and went to my job, and then returned home to fix supper. (Lubbock had a good bus system, which I used for all of my transportation.) Coming from a large family and a farm background, I was no stranger to hard work and responsibility, so I did not feel overloaded.

I also lived at two different boarding houses during college, Mrs. Davies', and Mrs. Blair's. I was living at Mrs. Blair's when I met Gid.

Financial independence meant the need for gainful employment. Once again, I was helped by my sister and contacts she had made a few years earlier. I was given a good reference for a local company called Broome Optical and began working for them, arranging appointments, meeting customers, and adjusting glasses frames. My employer, Mr. Broome, paid me six dollars a week and he also paid my fifty-dollar-per-semester college tuition. He was a very gracious and generous man. He had an older child who was disabled and invested both time and money in helping disabled children. His generous nature was also evidenced by the fact that, when I left for several months to be with my new husband, and later to have a baby, there was always a job waiting for me when I came back.

The McAffees, in addition to being my hosts, were customers of Broome. They took a special interest in me and came by from time to time to check on me during the times I was living elsewhere.

After getting married in New Orleans at Thanksgiving 1943, Gid and I came back to his West Texas home, Abernathy, and spent about six days with his parents before he shipped out to Arizona for training. Knowing that we could probably spend some time together on the East Coast before he went overseas, I did not re-enroll at Tech, but instead packed my things and prepared to move to New Jersey.

New Jersey, March 1944

Gid finished his training in Arizona and we traveled together by train to New Jersey in March 1944, which was to be our first time of any length together as a married couple. It was customary for people living in the vicinity of military installations to turn their homes into boarding houses, so it was not hard to find a place for the two of us to stay while we awaited his departure. We boarded with a Mrs. Anderson, along with five other army couples. The men were on duty at the base during many of the weekdays and spent the weekends at the house. We had kitchen privileges except on weekends, which was frustrating, because I really wanted to cook for Gid, and that was the only opportunity that I had to do so. One weekend, I got my wish when Mrs. Anderson told me that I could have the kitchen. I decided to make a pot of beef and vegetable soup-his favorite and my specialty.

Grocery stores did not sell meat at that time; you had to go to a meat market, and it was rationed. When I got to the local meat market the line extended about thirty feet out the door. By this time, I was pretty sure that I was pregnant, and as I moved into the store the aroma of fresh meat made me nauseous. I asked the next person in line to hold my place, excused myself, and found a place to discreetly toss my cookies, after which I came back and made my purchase. The soup turned out fine.

I have been asked if the news of my pregnancy was cause for celebration. The answer is no. In those days, the topic of pregnancy was kept low-key. In keeping with the tone of the times, I did not say much to anyone about my condition. Also, I knew that, when I informed my mother, she would not approve of my predicament—a pregnant young wife with a husband sailing off to fight in a war. I wasn't looking forward to having that discussion.

Good-Bye and Back Home, July 1944

The day finally came for my husband to ship out. The men were to travel by train to the harbor to board the Queen Mary, so the train station is where we said our goodbyes. It was very hard and there were few dry eyes among the wives and family members as the train left the station. I had become friends with several other wives and we all consoled one another other as the train left the station. After Gid was gone, I came back to the boarding house, packed my things, and prepared to move back to West Texas. One of Gid's buddies, Doughy Lockhart and his wife Beulah, lived in the house with us. Doughy was the supply officer for Gid's battalion, and the four of us had become close friends. Beulah owned a car and offered to drive me as far as her home in Red Oak, Iowa, so that part of my trip was made by car. From there, I caught a train to Wichita, Kansas, to visit my sister, Lois. The train was completely full and I had to sit on my suitcase in the restroom at the back of the car I was in. It was a long trip.

As I mentioned earlier, I was one of nine children. Of my seven brothers, five were in the service during World War II. Two brothers were air force pilots and one was a navy fighter pilot operating off a carrier in the Pacific who was just short of becoming an ace in a Grumman Hellcat when the war with Japan ended. Another was a sailor in the Pacific, and the last was a sergeant in the army. Thankfully, they all returned home safely.

Waiting

By the time I returned home from New Jersey as a married woman, I had been living on my own for quite a while and did not want to go back to the farm. It was now August 1944. I came back to Lubbock, moved into a duplex, and went back to work for Broome Optical. The other half of the duplex was occupied by two old-maid school teachers. When I submitted my rental application, the landlady told me that no children were allowed. I was not showing yet, so I took my chances and did not tell her that I was pregnant.

I had quite a few friends. To occupy our time, we got together almost every night and weekend and played Liverpool Rummy. I wrote to Gid regularly and got some letters back from him, but he was not able to communicate in much detail due to security regulations. I could tell that he was occupied with the duties at hand.

Motherhood

The McAffees came to see me at work from time to time and were especially attentive as my pregnancy progressed. My baby was due around the first of the year, and just before Christmas, Mrs. McAffee urged me to take a few days off work and move in with them until the baby was born and I could get back on my feet. I took her up on the offer, which turned out to be a wise decision.

My water broke at about midnight on December 31, while they were at a New Year's Eve party. When they came home, I told Mrs. McAffee what had happened. It was time to go to the hospital. Mr. McAffee helped me get into the car and drove to the hospital down nearly empty streets. I remember that it was snowing and he drove very carefully. By the time we arrived it was about 3:00 a.m. Gid III, was born at 5:30 in the morning, January 1, 1945. He was the first baby born in Lubbock County that year, an event that was covered in the local newspaper. Since the

Lubbock–Hale county line ran through the middle of Gid's home town, one of the local newspapers in Hale County also claimed him as their first New Year's baby.

My father and mother were still on the farm in Quitaque, about ninety miles away. As soon as I was released from the hospital, I moved back to my duplex and my mother moved in with me for a couple of weeks to help out. There had been a long—standing tradition for the local merchants in Lubbock to celebrate the birth of first baby of the New Year by giving free merchandise to the parents. This custom had fallen by the wayside during the war, but my mother, who could be quite forceful, decided that the birth of her grandson was cause for resurrecting the tradition, war or no war. She went to the local grocery store and harangued them until they coughed up two cases of Carnation milk. I guess it was a victory of sorts.

I stayed at the duplex for a few months, until the school teachers next door began to complain about the baby crying. The landlady told me that I would have to move out because of the rules concerning children in the units. I wanted to protest, but she had made the rules clear at the beginning, so I moved on.

I found a place to rent nearby, above a garage. After a few months, money began to run low, so I took the baby back to Quitaque to stay with my parents while I once again resumed my job at Broome Optical. I would work all week and, on Friday night, take the train home for the weekend. Sunday nights, I boarded the train and came back to Lubbock. This arrangement lasted until Gid came home from the war in December 1945. Thus, my son spent a good part of his first year of life with his grandparents. My parents, and especially my mother, adored him. As a result, among all of the grandkids who came along as the years went by, he was always their favorite.

My life as a serviceman's wife did not differ much from others, because almost everyone had a relative serving in the war effort, in one form or another. I did have one very personal experience related to my husband's service, however. One day in March 1945, my younger brother Dan had stopped by to visit. We were having coffee when all of a sudden I started crying. Puzzled, he asked what was wrong. "Something has happened to Gid," I replied. He thought I was a little crazy, but I got a telegram a few days later stating that Gid had been wounded in action. When he came home, we compared notes and the time of my premonition was the day and hour that he had been wounded the third time.

The time of his absence went by slowly, but again, the country was at war, so I was not alone. He was in my thoughts constantly, but I knew that worrying would not change anything, so I can't say that I worried about him. I did what I knew to do, spend time with friends and family, and make the best of things.

Reunited, December 1945

I was not quite ready for Gid's arrival the day and time that he finally came home. I had just moved and sent him a letter with my new address, but it had not caught up with him, so I did not know exactly when he would show up. He tracked down my new address, walked up the sidewalk, and knocked on the door. I answered the door, not knowing it was him, with my hair up in curlers. I really wanted to look good for him, but he caught me off guard. After being apart for eighteen months, it didn't really matter. He was still the same wonderful man that I had married two Thanksgivings before—a little the worse for wear, but that was certainly understandable. I was eager to begin our life together with the confidence that we would never have to be separated again.

We had actually not lived much of a "normal" life together, in spite of being married for more than two years. Our courtship was long distance, and he was so busy preparing to go overseas when we lived in New Jersey that we did not settle into much of a routine. Now we could be a married couple and resume growing our family.

We moved in with his parents and they began to look for a home in town, with the understanding that Gid's father, Gid, Sr., would retire and Gid would take over the farm. So, within a few months, we had our own place on the farm, in the house where Gid had been born and raised. Life was good.

Post War: More From Marie

The events of the war carried over into our lives for some time. One of my best and most loyal customers when I was working at

Broome Optical was a very nice couple in their fifties, Mr. and Mrs. Lit Moore, who also had a son in the army in Germany. They, like the McAffees, were protective of me, would not let anyone touch their glasses but me, and would come by the office from time to time just to visit and make sure I was doing alright. They made a point of visiting me when I was in the hospital with the baby, and they even brought me some hard candy, which was special because it was a valuable, hard-to-find commodity during the war.

One day not long after Gid had come home, I saw a picture of the Moore family in the Lubbock paper, which I pointed out to Gid, explaining that they had been a special couple who had sort of watched out for me while he was gone. He looked at the picture and exclaimed, "That's Kay Moore. We were in the hospital together in France." He told me the story and we made arrangements to get together. We had a great time and Gid enjoyed seeing his army buddy. Mrs. Moore was very enthusiastic about this being "the Lord's hand; we were watching out for you, and at the same time, Gid was taking care of Kay." I don't know why we had not made those connections before, but we hadn't.

Some of the post-war adjustments and experiences came from the stress of battle. Gid talked a lot about the men who didn't make it back. For about a year and a half, I would be awakened from time to time by the lieutenant barking orders to his men.

"Get down! Get down!"

"No, no, no. Don't move until I tell you to."

"Let's go! Move out!"

He never really woke up, so I just waited for the orders to subside and went back to sleep. I wasn't sure how to react, so we really did not discuss his dreams.

Not long after our second son, Tommy, was born, in the late spring of 1947, Gid began to have terrible stomach pains one afternoon. Dr. Williams, the local doctor, came out to the house, examined him, and said he was having an appendicitis attack and that we needed to get him to the hospital in Lubbock right away. He called and made arrangements for surgery while my father-in-law and I took Gid to the hospital, a drive of about twenty miles. He was wheeled into the operating room, which had an observation deck for medical students to use. The surgeon said we were welcome to observe the procedure if we wanted, so we took our seats while anesthesia was administered. After waiting to make sure that he was unconscious, the surgeon began to make an incision.

"Ouch, that hurts," Gid said.

The doctor administered another dose of anesthesia, waited and started again.

"Ouch, that hurts," Gid repeated.

The surgeon looked up at us and asked, "Was this boy in the war?"

"Yes he was," my father-in-law answered.

"Well, that explains it. We've found that a lot of these men have lived on such a high state of alert for so long that they have trained their bodies to resist losing consciousness. In some cases, it is almost impossible to knock them completely out."

He administered yet another dose of anesthesia and was able to complete the procedure without Gid waking up any more.

Chapter 17
After the War, and What it all Meant

As I had planned from the beginning, I resumed life on the farm. We raised cotton, some maize, wheat, and alfalfa on the three-quarters of a section that I had worked years before as a boy. It was, is, and always will be, home. Life as a West Texas farmer can be a challenge, but there is no place like it, and no place I would rather be. I had seen enough of the world in a two-year period that I had no desire to pack up and hit the open road. I told my wife that we could travel anywhere in the world, as long as we were home by sunset. The potential of reduced financial pressure that other employment might bring would be nice, but I liked the independence that farming afforded, and did not see any other realistic career options.

Our family grew to the point that we eventually had six children. We had plenty of friends, and, typical of small towns in the 50s and 60s, everyone shared common values and looked out for each other. All of my friends had grown up in the Great Depression and had learned to survive, and even be thankful for the basics of life—food, clothing, a roof overhead, and good health.

Abernathy certainly would not fit the definition of being a prosperous area, but people were content and complaints were few. Except for the single payday and unpredictability of the weather (a hailstorm or sandstorm could wipe out a crop in a matter of minutes), life on the farm near my West Texas home town was good.

Driving a tractor at three miles an hour for ten hours a day gives a person lots of time to think. I felt blessed, and wanted for nothing. As a matter of fact, I felt so blessed that my thinking morphed into a gnawing sense of obligation. I often felt that I had so much that I should be giving something to others. My life could have been snuffed out countless times, as had happened to so many of those around me, yet I was spared. Was I spared for a purpose?

167

Did not my survival against so many odds carry with it the inherent obligation to give something back to my fellow man?

I pondered these things for a long time but could not see an easy resolution, especially with the demands of a growing family and running a small farm. Then, out of the blue, in August 1958, an opportunity was dropped into my lap. One of my former high school classmates, Noel Johnson, had become superintendent of Abernathy schools. Noel had been a naval officer during the war and had gone into the teaching profession after returning to civilian life. His wife Wilma had been my steady girlfriend in high school. We had been serious enough that some mutual friends thought that we would end up husband and wife. The Johnsons were now among or our closest friends.

Noel called me one night during the second week in August and asked me if I could meet him at his office the next day. I doffed my overalls, put on a pair of khaki slacks, and drove our old Dodge pickup into town. He told me that the person he had contracted to teach high school math had informed him at the eleventh hour that he would not be able to fulfill his obligation, leaving Noel in a lurch. He had scoured the region, looking for unemployed math teachers, but came up empty-handed. Out of options, he decided to give me a call and see if I would like to try my hand at teaching. When I reminded him that I had not received my degree, he said he could pull strings to allow me to teach without a degree temporarily, and that, if this was something I wanted to pursue, I could continue to teach while completing required course work to earn my degree.

Marie and I talked it over and I said "Yes." Within a few weeks, I knew that I had found my calling. I still had farming in my blood, but the interaction with others, helping students, intellectual stimulation, and the professional environment made me feel like I had come home. Most of all, I found myself in a profession where the question of making a contribution was answered.

I soon found myself busier but more satisfied than ever. I enrolled in night classes at Texas Tech in Lubbock, contacted A&M, and they worked out a degree program that allowed me to earn my long-delayed diploma without repeating courses. Within a few months, I was teaching full-time, attending night classes, managing the farm, and reviewing summer school class offerings. I had a very dependable hired hand named Sam Betts, and my sons were old enough to put in a full day's work in the summer and work after classes during the school year. With no intentions of leaving or selling the farm, I didn't really change careers; I just added a new one.

After acquiring my college degree, I enrolled in a master's program in education at Texas Tech and was awarded that degree three years later.

After several years in the classroom, I became a principal and held several other administrative jobs until I was finally hired as superintendent of schools for the district. I held that position for four years and retired in 1986.

We kept the farm and in 1980 began to rent it out. As of this writing, my wife and I are both retired, living in the same house I was raised in, enjoying time with friends and family.

Reflections

In writing all of this down, I have found myself reliving many experiences—some good, some not so good. In particular, it is difficult to describe my feelings about all that I lived through during my fifteen months overseas. I would not say the feelings are good, because I endured many hardships and some very painful hours. Yet, intermingled with the painful were some light-hearted and certainly some rewarding moments. One cannot go through the real life-and-death trauma of combat without being profoundly impacted. Reflecting on the war seldom fails to evoke in me a wide range of thoughts and emotions. Though the stories related here took place more than sixty-five years ago, and the memories have mellowed with time, some scenes are still crystal clear. I have long since allowed emotions to surface, albeit privately, that I shut down when my troops and I were in the attack amidst barrages of artillery and mortar rounds. I have, over the years, tried to process things that I was not always able to fully understand or articulate. Many veterans find that they are not able to speak of their war experiences. Their war years are locked away and remain a mystery to friends and family, oftentimes for life. To keep the things I saw that affected me down to the very marrow of my bones, walled off as if they never happened, would have been more stressful for me personally than talking about them. What happened happened, for better or worse. We all deal with it in our own way.

Growing up as a somewhat naïve farm boy, near a quiet country town, then being hurled headlong into an insanely loud, bloody, cold-hearted war machine broadened my perspective greatly. It prompted me to reconsider many of the assumptions I lived with, especially in terms of the nature of man. On the battlefield, I saw my fellow man at his very best, but also at his very worst. I saw the results of extreme cruelty by some and witnessed great kindness and sacrifice by others. After much thought, I concluded that I could choose to dwell on the unfairness of war and the darkness I saw that could arise out of men's souls, or I could focus on the brave, sacrificial acts of many that came out of a noble place that also resides in men. While I have seen first-hand that we are capable of carrying out terribly evil acts, I believe that there is inherent good in every person. Therefore, I decided long ago to do my best to convert my perceptions into actions, to be an influence for good in my environment and in the way I relate to others.

Largely because of my war experiences, I mentally commissioned myself to be an agent of looking for and calling forth the good in my fellow man. My career in education has been fertile ground for fulfilling this calling, and, as such, has been very rewarding. Hopefully, I have been able to help those who came into my sphere of influence to see themselves as valuable, significant individuals, able to make a contribution in their corner of the world, however large or small it may be. I may never have come to this place had I not endured the hardships and witnessed the extreme good and bad perpetrated by my fellow man. Who knows?

Finally, when I sort out my feelings about what I have seen, what I have learned, what was, and what might have been, one thing stands tall above all else, and that is a sense of pride: pride in my fellow servicemen and pride in my country. In my early adult years, America joined together in fighting for a just cause. I am proud to have been a part of it. I fought and bled alongside a group of ordinary, everyday men who answered the call to lay their lives on the line for this cause. I am proud of my country and I am proud to be numbered among those who served.

We did a good thing.

Dear Reader,

If you enjoyed this book from Pacifica Military History and IPS Books, please visit our website at **http://www.PacificaMilitary.com**, where many other books of similar high quality are offered in printed or electronic versions. The site also offers a *free* book-length sampler with excerpts from most of our active titles.

Your patronage is deeply appreciated.

Pacifica Military History

CPSIA information can be obtained at www.ICGtesting.com
Printed in the USA
LVOW10s0129281013

358792LV00001B/5/P